National 5
English
Practice Papers for SQA Exams

Colin Eckford

Contents

HODDER
GIBSON
AN HACHETTE UK COMPANY

The Publishers would like to thank the following for permission to reproduce copyright material:

Critical Essay supplementary marking grid on pages 112, 140 and 166 reproduced by permission copyright © Scottish Qualifications Authority.

Acknowledgements: please refer to page 167.

Every effort has been made to trace all copyright holders, but if any have been inadvertently overlooked the Publishers will be pleased to make the necessary arrangements at the first opportunity.

Although every effort has been made to ensure that website addresses are correct at time of going to press, Hodder Gibson cannot be held responsible for the content of any website mentioned in this book. It is sometimes possible to find a relocated web page by typing in the address of the home page for a website in the URL window of your browser.

Hachette UK's policy is to use papers that are natural, renewable and recyclable products and made from wood grown in sustainable forests. The logging and manufacturing processes are expected to conform to the environmental regulations of the country of origin.

Orders: please contact Bookpoint Ltd, 130 Park Drive, Milton Park, Abingdon, Oxon OX14 4SB. Telephone: (44) 01235 827720. Fax: (44) 01235 400454. Lines are open 9.00–5.00, Monday to Saturday, with a 24-hour message answering service. Visit our website at www.hoddereducation.co.uk. Hodder Gibson can be contacted direct on: Tel: 0141 333 4650; Fax: 0141 404 8188;
email: hoddergibson@hodder.co.uk

© Colin Eckford 2016

First published in 2016 by
Hodder Gibson, an imprint of Hodder Education,
An Hachette UK Company
211 St Vincent Street
Glasgow G2 5QY

Impression number	5 4 3 2 1
Year	2020 2019 2018 2017 2016

Cover photo © Stock Connection Blue/Alamy Stock Photo
Typeset in DIN Regular, 12/14.4 pts. by Aptara Inc.
Printed and bound by CPI Group (UK) Ltd, Croydon, CR0 4YY

A catalogue record for this title is available from the British Library

Introduction

National 5 English

The course

The National 5 English course aims to enable you to develop the ability to:

- listen, talk, read and write, as appropriate to purpose, audience and context
- understand, analyse and evaluate texts, including Scottish texts, as appropriate to purpose and audience in the contexts of literature, language and media
- create and produce texts, as appropriate to purpose, audience and context
- apply knowledge and understanding of language.

How the award is graded

The grade you finally get for National 5 English depends on three things:

- the two internal Unit Assessments you do in school or college: 'Analysis and Evaluation' and 'Creation and Production'; these don't count towards the final grade, but you must have passed them before you can get a final grade
- your Portfolio of Writing – this is submitted in April for marking by SQA and counts for 30% of your final grade
- the two exams you sit in May – that's what this book is all about.

The exams

Reading for Understanding, Analysis and Evaluation

- Exam time: 1 hour
- Total marks: 30
- Weighting in final grade: 30%
- What you have to do: read a passage and answer questions about it.

Critical Reading

- Exam time: 1 hour 30 minutes
- Total marks: 40
- Weighting in final grade: 40%
- What you have to do: Section 1: read an extract from one of the Scottish Texts which are set for National 5 and answer questions about it; Section 2: write an essay about a work of literature you have studied during your course.

Reading for Understanding, Analysis and Evaluation

Two important tips to start with

- Since there will always be a question asking you to summarise some or all of the passage, it is really important to read the whole passage before you even look at the questions. Doing this will give you a chance to get a rough idea of the main ideas in the passage, and you can add to this as you work your way through the questions.
- Pay close attention to the number of marks available for each question and make sure your answer is appropriate for the number of marks. In most questions, you will get 1 mark for each correct point.

Questions which ask for understanding

- Keep your answers fairly short and pay attention to the number of marks available.
- In most questions there is an instruction to 'use your own words' or to 'use your own words as far as possible'. This means you mustn't just copy chunks from the passage – you have to show that you understand what it means by rephrasing it in your own words.

Questions about language features

- This type of question will ask you to comment on features such as word choice, sentence structure or imagery.
- You should pick out a relevant language feature and make a valid comment about its impact. Try to make your comments as specific as possible and avoid vague comments (like 'It is a good word to use because it gives me a clear picture of what the writer is saying'). Some hints:
  - **word choice**: Always try to pick a single word and then give its connotations, i.e. what it **suggests**.
  - **sentence structure**: Don't just name the feature – try to explain what effect it achieves **in that particular sentence**.
  - **imagery**: Try to explain what the image means **literally** and then go on to explain what the writer is trying to say by using that image.

Summary questions

- Make sure you follow the instruction about what you are to summarise (the question will be as helpful as possible).
- Stick to main ideas; avoid unimportant points and never include examples.
- Make sure you earn all the marks available for the question.

Critical Reading

Section 1 – Scottish Text

The most important thing to remember here is that there are two very different types of question to be answered:

- three or four questions (for a total of 12 marks) which focus entirely on the extract
- one question (for 8 marks) which requires knowledge of the whole text (or of another poem or short story by the same writer).

The first type of question will often ask you to use the same type of close textual analysis skills that you used in the Reading part of your Analysis and Evaluation Unit. There can also be a question asking for the type of summary skills you're used to in the Reading part of the exam. The golden rule is to read each question very carefully and do exactly as instructed.

The second type of question will ask you to make connections between the extract and the rest of the text (drama and novels) or between the extract and another text by the same writer (short stories and poems). The marker will be looking for three things:

- identification of 'commonality' as specified in the question (for 2 marks)
- at least one relevant reference to and comment on the extract (for 2 marks)
- at least two relevant references to and comments on the rest of the text (or other poems or short stories) (for 4 marks).

Your answer to this question can be in bullet points or in the form of a 'mini-essay'. Good marks can be obtained using either approach. You should decide which method you are most comfortable with, and use it confidently.

A final bit of advice for the Scottish Text question: when you see the extract in the exam paper, don't get too excited just because you recognise it (you certainly should recognise it if you've studied properly!). And even if you've answered questions on that extract in practice tests, remember that the questions in the exam are likely to be different, so stay alert.

Section 2 – Critical Essay

A common mistake when writing Critical Essays is relying too heavily on ideas and whole paragraphs you have used in practice essays and trying to use them for the question you have chosen in the exam. The trick is to come to the exam with lots of ideas and thoughts about at least one of the texts you have studied and use these to tackle the question you choose from the exam paper. You mustn't use the exam question as an excuse to trot out an answer you've prepared in advance.

Structure

Every good essay has a structure, but there is no 'correct' structure, no magic formula that the examiners are looking for. It's **your** essay, so structure it the way **you** want. As long as you're answering the question all the way through, then you'll be fine.

Relevance

Be relevant to the question **all the time** – not just in the first and last paragraphs.

Central concerns

Try to make sure your essay shows that you have thought about and understood the central concerns of the text, i.e. what it's 'about' – the ideas and themes the writer is exploring in the text.

Quotations

In essays on poetry and drama, you're expected to quote from the text – but never fall into the trap of learning a handful of quotations and forcing them all into the essay regardless of the question you're answering. In essays on novels and short stories, quotation is much less important, and you can usually show your knowledge more effectively by referring in detail to what happens in key sections of the novel or the short story.

Techniques

You are expected to show an understanding of how various literary techniques (such as setting, characterisation, etc.) work within a text, but simply naming them will not get you credit, and structuring your essay around techniques rather than around relevant ideas in the text is not a good idea.

Further reading

- Look on the SQA website for the Course Report for National 5 English, which is published every year (usually in October) and contains very useful comments from the Principal Assessor on candidates' performance in that year's exam.
- The book *How to Pass: National 5 English* by David Swinney (Hodder Gibson, ISBN 978-1-4441-8209-5) provides a detailed guide to all aspects of the course. It is endorsed by SQA.

Good luck!

Remember that the awards for passing National 5 English are well worth it. Your pass will help you get the future you want for yourself. In the exam, be confident in your own ability – if you're not sure how to answer a question trust your instincts and just give it a go anyway. Keep calm and don't panic! Good luck!

Revision grid

Reading for Understanding, Analysis and Evaluation

The grid below will help you focus on the different types of questions that feature in the RUAE paper. You can tick them off as you work through this book.

Question Type	Paper A		Paper B		Paper C	
Understanding	2,6,8,9		1,4,6,8		1,3,5,6	
Summary	5		5		4	
Analysis	3,4,7		2,3,7		2,7,8	
Evaluation	1		9		9	

Critical Reading

It is not possible to focus in the same way on the skills for Critical Reading, but the grid below will allow you to keep a record of which Scottish Text examples and Critical Essays you have worked on.

Scottish text

Name of text	Date completed:		
	Paper A	Paper B	Paper C

Critical essay

Name of text	Paper	Question	Date

National 5
English

HODDER
GIBSON
LEARN MORE

Paper 1: Reading for Understanding, Analysis and Evaluation

Duration: 1 hour

Total marks: 30

Attempt ALL questions.

Write your answers clearly in the answer booklet provided. In the answer booklet you must clearly identify the question number you are attempting.

Use **blue** or **black** ink.

Before leaving the examination room you must give your answer booklet to the Invigilator; if you do not you may lose all the marks for this paper.

Sport is here to stay

At the weekend, I watched a fair bit of sport. I watched the cricket on Sky Sports Ashes, the Manchester United v Tottenham Hotspur game on Sky Sports 1, *Match of the Day* on BBC One, a bit of the *Football League Tonight* show on Channel 5 and the headlines on Sky Sports News at Ten. I could also have watched Sky Sports F1; BT Sport 1 and 2; Eurosport 1 and 2; MUTV,

5 Chelsea TV, Premier Sports, Racing UK, BoxNation, and dozens of other digital channels devoted to live, recorded and highlighted sport.

The pre-eminent position of sport in our media-dominated culture is well established. But it is worth taking a step back to see just how unexpected this development has been. It is remarkable to note that not a single English top-flight football match was broadcast before

10 Christmas in the 1985–86 season, owing to a dispute between the FA and TV stations. There was only a small outcry from the public. Today, there might have been rioting.

If you rewind just a little farther back, the cultural significance of sport today seems even more striking. In the middle of the 19th century, the Olympic Games didn't exist and neither did the World Cup. There were almost no governing bodies.

15 As for most of the previous 15 centuries, sport was a fringe activity out of keeping with religious sensibilities, which regarded kicking and hitting balls as a frivolous pastime. The bulk of individuals in the western world went through life without any conception that these invented games would one day come to dominate global consciousness.

When I was in my teens, it wasn't just the history of sport that looked bleak, the future did as

20 well. When I went to a careers evening at school and said that I wanted to become a sports journalist, the adviser spluttered. She doubted that sport would be big enough to support

such a career. She pointed to the growth in technology, video games, virtual reality and a host of other things that were set to transform leisure time. 'I doubt many people will be watching sport 20 years from now,' she said.

25 This wasn't just her view, it was the consensus among many social commentators. The idea that sport might soon become dominant and pre-eminent in the media would have been laughed at. That is why the trajectory of sport's growth is worth reflecting upon.

It is not only represented in the proliferation of TV channels, it is also stimulating this proliferation. 'Premium sports content' drives subscriptions. The jostle between BT and Sky
30 over football rights (reaching fever pitch in advertising spend at present) is where the war over broadband may be won and lost.

The possibility that Google, Netflix and the like will start to bid for premium sports rights is predicated upon the same logic. These corporate giants know that if they wish to build new markets (and cut the legs from under traditional players, such as Sky), they have to use sport as a Trojan
35 horse. In a world where sport is the dominant feature of social interaction, there is no other way.

There has been a proliferation in radio stations (such as talkSPORT, Radio 5 live and sports extra) too, along with hundreds of podcasts and blogs. Far from being replaced by new technologies, as my careers adviser predicted, sport has colonised them. Football is the most prevalent theme on Twitter. And it is what people want to watch on a growing list of devices,
40 whether tablets, laptops or, increasingly, the latest generation of smartphones.

Simultaneously, the social function of sport is solidifying. It is the chosen vehicle to break the ice when we (particularly men) talk to each other, whether at an office meeting or wherever else. It is pretty much the only activity that allows large sections of society to come together in a shared experience, such as when your home country is playing a World Cup match.

45 How did this astonishing transformation in the meaning of sport come about? Perhaps the crucial turning point came with the project to redefine sport's moral status in the Victorian era. The idea that games such as rugby, football and cricket help young people to respect rules and develop character created an impetus to codify games and establish functioning governing bodies, which spread throughout the empire.

50 But where next? When I started in sports journalism, I wondered if the bubble would soon burst. I looked for a tipping point, subtle signs that the infatuation was petering out. Today, however, I suspect that sport is here to stay as a cultural giant. This is not a bubble, it is something more permanent. Instead of interpreting the past century and a half as an aberration, it is possible to see the centuries beforehand as the true anomaly.

55 When you take the long view, the present status of sport seems entirely natural. Consider that the Ancient Olympics, the most significant human festival of antiquity, lasted, without interruption, for 1,170 years. This longevity has no precedent. The festival, to which spectators flocked from throughout the Greek world, was not interrupted by pestilence, by war, and certainly not by apathy.

60 This suggests that sport will sustain its present standing because, as with the ancient festivals, it speaks to something permanent in the human psyche. No amount of technological, economic, religious or social change will eradicate this, except temporarily, as in the medieval period. These unscripted sporting dramas move and inspire us. They evoke themes of competition, teamwork and rivalry, which are central to the human condition. They
65 help people to escape the humdrum and ordinary.

Sport is here to stay.

Matthew Syed, in The Times

Questions

MARKS

1   Explain fully why the first paragraph (lines 1–6) is an effective opening to the passage as a whole.

3

2   Look at lines 7–18, and then explain **in your own words four** on ways in which the importance of sport has changed over the years.

4

3   Look at lines 19–27. Explain what the careers adviser's attitude was to sports journalism, and how one example of the writer's **word choice** makes this attitude clear.

3

4   Look at lines 28–35, and then explain how **two** examples of the writer's **word choice** demonstrate how fierce the competition is among TV channels.

4

5   Look at lines 36–44, and then explain using **your own words** as far as possible **four** pieces of evidence the writer gives to show that the careers adviser was wrong about people's interest in sport.

4

6   Look at lines 45–49, and then explain **in your own words** the importance of the 'Victorian era' in changing attitudes to sport.

2

7   Look at lines 50–54, and then explain how two examples of the language used (such as **word choice, sentence structure** or **imagery**) demonstrate the writer's feelings about sport.

4

8   Look at lines 55–59, and then explain in **your own words three** reasons why the writer refers to the Ancient Olympics to support his argument.

3

9   Look at lines 60–66, and then explain **in your own words three** reasons why, according to the writer, sport is important to us.

3

[End of question paper]

Paper 2: Critical Reading

Duration: 90 minutes

Total marks: 40

SECTION 1 – Scottish Text – 20 marks

Read an extract from a Scottish text you have previously studied.

Choose ONE text from either

Part A – Drama   Pages 7–11

or

Part B – Prose   Pages 12–18

or

Part C – Poetry   Pages 19–24

Attempt ALL the questions for your chosen text.

SECTION 2 – Critical Essay – 20 marks

Attempt ONE question from the following genres – Drama, Prose, Poetry, Film and Television Drama, or Language.

Your answer must be on a different genre from that chosen in Section 1.

You should spend approximately 45 minutes on each Section.

Write your answers clearly in the answer booklet provided. In the answer booklet you must clearly identify the question number you are attempting.

Use **blue** or **black** ink.

Before leaving the examination room you must give your answer booklet to the Invigilator; if you do not you may lose all the marks for this paper.

Section 1 – Scottish Text – 20 marks

Part A – Scottish Text – Drama

Text 1 – Drama

If you choose this text you may not attempt a question on Drama in Section 2.

Read the extract below and then attempt the following questions.

Bold Girls by Rona Munro

The extract is from Scene One. The women recall the night Cassie's husband was arrested.

	NORA:	Oh do you remember the night they took Joe? You should've seen me, Marie.
	CASSIE:	She was something that night, Andytown's own Incredible Hulk, 'Don't get me angry'!
	NORA:	Well Marie, there was wee Cassie —
5	CASSIE:	Wee? I'm wee again am I?
	NORA:	—just a week out the hospital with the stitches still in from the section that gave us Teresa, and I open my door and here she is running up the road —
	CASSIE:	That was when we had our own house, you know, at the end there —
	NORA:	Squealing 'Mummy! Mummy!' —
10	CASSIE:	—one hand clutching my stomach 'cause I'm sure the whole lot's going to fall out.
	NORA:	—'Mummy! Mummy! They're taking Joe!' Well I just felt my blood rise —
	CASSIE:	She was a lioness. She was.
	NORA:	—I marched back up the road and here they were, dragging the poor man
15		out of his own house without even a pair of shoes on his feet —
	CASSIE:	He'd been snoring away in front of the football, toasting his toes, with a pie in one hand and a can in the other.
	NORA:	Sure he'd not been ready for any trouble; why would he be?
	CASSIE:	And the rest of them are throwing everything every which way and all over the
20		house and the baby's screaming and the child's calling for her daddy —
	NORA:	And he keeps his hand tight round this pie the whole time they were dragging him away. And I goes up to this big RUC man and I says —
	CASSIE:	She picked the biggest.
	NORA:	I says, 'What's the charges? Where's your warrants?'
25	CASSIE:	And he's peering down at her like he's a mountain and she's a beetle at the bottom of it.
	NORA:	And he says 'And who are you?' And I says, 'I'm that boy's mother-in-law, and before you take him you'll have to answer to me!'
	CASSIE:	Can you beat it, Marie?
30	NORA:	And he says, 'You get out of our way Mrs or it'll be the worse for you.'
	CASSIE:	He didn't say it as nice as that Mummy, there was a few fucking old ...

	NORA:	We do not need to use language like that Cassie! 'Out the way or it'll be the worse for you,' he says. Oh he was a big bastard Marie. 'Oh,' I says, 'Oh would you strike a woman that could be your own mother? Would you
35		now?' (*She starts to laugh*)
	MARIE:	What happened?
	CASSIE:	Wallop! Knocked her straight through the hedge.
	NORA:	(*still laughing*) Would you hit a mother? Sure I got my answer on the end of his fist.
40	CASSIE:	Nearly choked on her false teeth.
	NORA:	I did.
	CASSIE:	I didn't know which of them to go to first, Joe, or Mummy in the hedge with her little legs waving in the air.
	NORA:	(*wiping her eyes, still laughing*) Oh – oh but that was a terrible night.

Questions

MARKS

1 Look at lines 1–13.

   a) By referring closely to **two** examples from these lines, show how Cassie's admiration for Nora is conveyed.

                                             4

   b) Explain how the dramatist conveys the liveliness of the dialogue in these lines.

                                             2

2 Explain **one** way in which the language of lines 14–20 conveys how fast-moving the incident was.

                                           2

3 Look at lines 21–44. Explain how the dramatist creates humour in the way Cassie and Nora recall the event.

                                           4

4 By referring to the extract and to elsewhere in the play, show how the women's lives are affected by 'The Troubles'.

                                           8

    OR

Text 2 – Drama

If you choose this text you may not attempt a question on Drama in Section 2.

Read the extract below and then attempt the following questions.

Sailmaker by Alan Spence

The extract is from Act Two. Davie arrives home from the pub.

	DAVIE:	(*Noticing* ALEC) Yawright son?
	ALEC:	(*Not looking up*) Aye.
	DAVIE:	Ach aye. Yirra good boy. What ye readin?
	ALEC:	A book.
5	DAVIE:	Naw! *Whit* book!

	ALEC:	David Copperfield. Got an exam next week.
	DAVIE:	Dickens, eh? Now yer talkin. Ah've read aw his books. The lot. Got them all out the library. Used tae read a lot ye know. Dickens is the greatest. David Copperfield is it?
10	ALEC:	That's what ah said.
	DAVIE:	Mr Micawber. Somethin'll turn up, eh?
		Income twenty pounds, expenditure nineteen pounds nineteen and six: result happiness.
		Income twenty pounds, expenditure twenty pounds and sixpence: result …
15		(*Shrugs*)
		Not to worry.
		Hey, ah got ye crisps. Bottle ae Irn Bru. (*Puts them on table*)
	ALEC:	(*Grudging*) Thanks.
	DAVIE:	Any chance ae a cuppa tea?
20	ALEC:	There's some left in the pot. (DAVIE *pours dregs*)
	DAVIE:	(*Sings*)
		Where the blue of the night
		Meets the gold of the day
		(*To* ALEC) Cheer up. (*No response*) C'mon. (*Spars*)
25	ALEC:	Chuck it will ye!
	DAVIE:	Torn face.
	ALEC:	Ah didnae know where ye wur.
	DAVIE:	Och …
	ALEC:	Might have been under a bus or anythin.
30	DAVIE:	(*Sighs*) Look. Ah'm sorry, awright? Just … wan a these things, ye know.
	ALEC:	Aye ah know.
	DAVIE:	Good company. Nae harm in it. Didnae even have a lot tae drink. It's just good tae relax.
		Wee refreshment. Ach aye. The patter was good tae.
35		Kenny's a great Burns man. Could recite Tam O'Shanter tae ye just like that! Yer sittin talkin away and he'll come out wi a line fae it.
		Fast by an ingle, bleezing finely
		Wi reamin swats that drank divinely
		Great stuff eh? Poetry!
40		Reamin swats!
		Anythin for eatin?
	ALEC:	Naw.
	DAVIE:	Nothin?
	ALEC:	Not a thing.
45	DAVIE:	What about that tin a soup?
	ALEC:	Ah had it for ma tea.
	DAVIE:	Oh aye. An the creamed rice?

	ALEC:	Ah ate that tae.
50	DAVIE:	Themorra ah'll get a nice bit steak. Have it wi chips. Fried tomatoes! Is there no even any bread?
	ALEC:	Nothin.
	DAVIE:	Can ah take a couple ae yer crisps?
	ALEC:	Help yerself.
55	DAVIE:	Just a couple. (*Eats crisps, swigs Irn Bru from bottle*) Reamin swats! There was this lassie there. In the company like. Peggy her name was. Friend ae Kenny's.
		Helluva nice tae talk tae. Know what ah mean? Just a really nice person.
	ALEC:	Oh aye. (*Bangs down book*)

Questions

MARKS

5   Identify **four** ways by which the dramatist makes it clear in lines 1–25 that Alec is annoyed with his father.

4

6   By referring to **two** examples in lines 26–41, explain how the way Davie speaks is typical of someone who is slightly drunk.

4

7   Show how the tension between Alec and his father is conveyed by the way they speak in lines 42–58.

4

8   Do you think Davie is a good parent or not? By referring to the extract and to elsewhere in the play, show how the dramatist makes you feel this way.

8

OR

Text 3 – Drama

If you choose this text you may not attempt a question on Drama in Section 2.

Read the extract below and then attempt the following questions.

Tally's Blood by Ann Marie Di Mambro

The extract is from Act Two, Scene Five. Rosinella confronts Lucia over Hughie's letter.

	ROSINELLA:	What's this, eh? He's writing to you now, eh?
	Rosinella opens it, takes it out.	
	ROSINELLA:	I knew it. It's a letter.
	She looks at it: frustrated because she can't read: thrusts it back at Lucia.	
5	ROSINELLA:	What's it say?
	LUCIA:	I don't know – it doesn't matter. I'll just chuck it.
	ROSINELLA:	I want to know what it says. Read it for me.
	LUCIA:	Auntie Rosinella, I don't know what's wrong with you these days.
	ROSINELLA:	Just read it.

Lucia starts to read letter: she has to think on her feet.

LUCIA: It's just ... just a letter.

ROSINELLA: What's it say?

LUCIA: It just says ... it just says ... Have I heard the new Guy Mitchell ...? It's really good ... he says ... and eh ... Would I ask my Uncle Massimo to get it for the juke box ...? Because he thinks it would be good ... for the customers ... So he does ... and so do I ... as well ... I think so too.

ROSINELLA: I don't believe you.

LUCIA: No, it is good. You not heard it? (*Sings/tries to cajole*) 'I never felt more like singing the blues, 'cause I never thought that I'd ever lose your love, dear. You got me singing the blues. I never felt more like ...'

ROSINELLA: Give me that. (*Grabs letter*)

LUCIA: (*Pleading*) Auntie Rosinella.

ROSINELLA: Don't you 'Auntie Rosinella' me. I didn't want to have to do this but you're making me. I want you to stay away from that Hughie Devlin, you hear?

LUCIA: But why?

ROSINELLA: I don't want you seeing him.

LUCIA: Hughie's my pal.

ROSINELLA: I don't want you talking to him.

LUCIA: I don't understand.

ROSINELLA: Just stay away.

LUCIA: I won't. You can't make me.

ROSINELLA: Alright then, lady, I'll fix you. I'll get rid of him.

LUCIA: (*Shocked*) You wouldn't.

ROSINELLA: I would in a minute. Jumped up wee piece of nothing thinks because he works here he can look at you. Him?

LUCIA: You'd do that to Hughie?

ROSINELLA: And you'd thank me for it one day. You think I brought you up to throw yourself away on the likes of him?

LUCIA: I can't believe you're saying this. (*A beat*) You've changed, Auntie Rosinella.

Questions

MARKS

9 Explain how the language used in lines 1–12 conveys Rosinella's hostility towards Lucia. 4

10 Explain how the way Lucia speaks in lines 13–20 makes it clear she is making up a story on the spot. 4

11 Explain how **two** examples of Rosinella's language in lines 21–39 make clear her low opinion of Hughie. 4

12 By referring to the extract and to elsewhere in the play, show how the relationship between Lucia and Hughie develops. 8

Section 1 – Scottish Text – 20 marks

Part B – Scottish Text – Prose

Text 1 – Prose

If you choose this text you may not attempt a question on Prose in Section 2.

Read the extract below and then attempt the following questions.

The Cone-Gatherers by Robin Jenkins

The extract is from Chapter 6, at the conclusion of the deer drive. Calum has just thrown himself at the injured deer.

While Captain Forgan, young Roderick, and Lady Runcie-Campbell stood petrified by this sight, Duror followed by his dogs came leaping out of the woods. He seemed to be laughing in some kind of berserk joy. There was a knife in his hand. His mistress shouted to him: what it was she did not know herself, and he never heard. Rushing upon the stricken deer and the
5   frantic hunchback, he threw the latter off with furious force, and then, seizing the former's head with one hand cut its throat savagely with the other. Blood spouted. Lady Runcie-Campbell closed her eyes. Captain Forgan shook his head slightly in some kind of denial. Roderick screamed at Duror. Tulloch had gone running over to Calum.

The deer was dead, but Duror did not rise triumphant; he crouched beside it, on his knees,
10   as if he was mourning over it. His hands were red with blood; in one of them he still held the knife.

There were more gunshots and shouts further down the ride.

It was Tulloch who hurried to Duror to verify or disprove the suspicion that had paralysed the others.

15   He disproved it. Duror was neither dead nor hurt.

Duror muttered something, too much of a mumble to be understood. His eyes were shut. Tulloch bent down to sniff; but he was wrong, there was no smell of whisky, only of the deer's sweat and blood. All the same, he thought, Duror had the appearance of a drunk man, unshaven, slack-mouthed, mumbling, rather glaikit.

20   Lady Runcie-Campbell came forward, with involuntary grimaces of distaste. She avoided looking at the hunchback, seated now against the bole of a tree, sobbing like a child, his face smeared with blood.

'Has he hurt himself?' she asked of Tulloch.

'I don't think so, my lady. He seems to have collapsed.'

25   Graham came panting down the ride.

His mistress turned round and saw him.

'Oh, Graham,' she said, 'please be so good as to drag this beast away.'

Graham glanced at deer and keeper. Which beast, your ladyship? he wanted to ask. Instead, he caught the deer by a hind leg and pulled it along the grass, leaving a trail of blood.

30 She turned back to Duror, now leaning against Tulloch.

'Have we nothing to wipe his face with?' she murmured peevishly.

Her brother was first to offer his handkerchief. With it Tulloch dabbed off the blood.

Questions

13 Show how the writer's use of language in lines 1–8 creates a dramatic scene.   4

14 By referring to lines 9–22, explain in your own words what makes Duror's behaviour appear to be out of the ordinary. You should make **four** key points.   4

15 By referring to lines 23–32, explain what impressions the writer creates of Lady Runcie-Campbell.   4

16 By referring to the extract and to elsewhere in the novel, show how the writer creates a contrast between Calum and Duror.   8

OR

Text 2 – Prose

If you choose this text you may not attempt a question on Prose in Section 2.

Read the extract below and then attempt the following questions.

The Testament of Gideon Mack by James Robertson

The extract is from Chapter 33. Elsie has just left the Manse after refusing to believe what Gideon tells her about the Stone.

A crisis was upon me. I was sweating, seething with energy. If I didn't do something the energy would burst out of me and leave me wrecked on the floor. My left arm was twitching as if in contact with an electric fence. I wanted to go to the Stone, yet at the same time was afraid to go. It seemed to me that the Stone had provoked this crisis, had engineered it in
5   some way. I paced round the manse, in and out of every room, up and down the stairs. I'd just decided to get changed and head off for a long run, to try to calm down, when the bell rang again. I thought Elsie must have come back and rushed to the front door. A car had pulled up in the drive, but not Elsie's. It was Lorna Sprott.

'Gideon,' Lorna said. 'I've been at the museum. I missed the exhibition opening but I've had a
10   good look round.' Something in my expression stopped her. 'Is this an awkward moment?'

'Actually, I was about to go for a run.'

'You wouldn't like to come for a walk instead? I've got Jasper in the car. I was thinking we might go to the Black Jaws.'

I opened my mouth to make an excuse, but she didn't notice.

15   'The exhibition surprised me,' she said. 'I didn't think it would be my cup of tea at all, and I can't say I understood everything, but it was quite thought-provoking. I saw old Menteith's

study and listened to you reading while I was looking down through that window. That's what put me in mind to go to the Black Jaws, the real place. I haven't been there for ages, and Jasper could do with a change from the beach.'

20 She looked pleadingly at me. How could I resist? Lorna stood on the step, inexorable and solid, and I knew I'd never get rid of her. Even if I slammed the door in her face she wouldn't leave me alone. I imagined her scraping and chapping at the windows until I let her in. 'Wait a minute,' I said, and went to get my boots and a jacket.

Perhaps I was meant to go for a walk with Lorna, to talk to her about what was going on.
25 Perhaps the Stone was wielding some strange power over events and had brought her to my door at this moment. In the minute or two it took me to get ready I made a decision. I would go with Lorna to the Black Jaws and, depending on how things went, I would swear her to secrecy, take her to Keldo Woods, and show her the Stone. I could trust her thus far, I knew. If Lorna acknowledged that the Stone existed, then I would know I was neither hallucinating nor
30 mad and I would go to Elsie and John. I would confront them with the misery and mockery of our lives and ask them to have the courage, with me, to change them. If, on the other hand, Lorna could not see the Stone, then I would have to admit that what Elsie had said was true, that I needed help.

Questions

MARKS

17 Show how **two** examples of the writer's language in lines 1–8 illustrate the idea that Gideon is in a 'crisis'. — 4

18 By referring to lines 9–23, explain **two** impressions the reader is given of Lorna's character. — 4

19 By referring to lines 24–33, show that Gideon's thinking is both rational **and** irrational. — 4

20 By referring to the extract and to elsewhere in the novel, show how the writer explores Gideon's relationships with women. (You should refer in your answer to at least **two** female characters.) — 8

OR

Text 3 – Prose

If you choose this text you may not attempt a question on Prose in Section 2.

Read the extract below and then attempt the following questions.

Kidnapped by Robert Louis Stevenson

The extract is from Chapter 24 – The Flight in the Heather: The Quarrel. *David and Alan leave Cluny's Cage and then follow the gillie's suggested route.*

We set forth accordingly by this itinerary; and for the best part of three nights travelled on eerie mountains and among the well-heads of wild rivers; often buried in mist, almost continually blown and rained upon, and not once cheered by any glimpse of sunshine. By day,

we lay and slept in the drenching heather; by night, incessantly clambered upon breakneck
5   hills and among rude crags. We often wandered; we were often so involved in fog, that we
must lie quiet till it lightened. A fire was never to be thought of. Our only food was drammach
and a portion of cold meat that we had carried from the Cage; and as for drink, Heaven knows
we had no want of water.

This was a dreadful time, rendered the more dreadful by the gloom of the weather and the
10   country. I was never warm; my teeth chattered in my head; I was troubled with a very sore
throat, such as I had on the isle; I had a painful stitch in my side, which never left me; and
when I slept in my wet bed, with the rain beating above and the mud oozing below me, it was
to live over again in fancy the worst part of my adventures—to see the tower of Shaws lit by
lightning, Ransome carried below on the men's backs, Shuan dying on the round-house floor,
15   or Colin Campbell grasping at the bosom of his coat. From such broken slumbers, I would
be aroused in the gloaming, to sit up in the same puddle where I had slept, and sup cold
drammach; the rain driving sharp in my face or running down my back in icy trickles; the mist
enfolding us like as in a gloomy chamber—or perhaps, if the wind blew, falling suddenly apart
and showing us the gulf of some dark valley where the streams were crying aloud.

20   The sound of an infinite number of rivers came up from all round. In this steady rain the
springs of the mountain were broken up; every glen gushed water like a cistern; every stream
was in high spate, and had filled and overflowed its channel. During our night tramps, it was
solemn to hear the voice of them below in the valleys, now booming like thunder, now with an
angry cry.

25   During all these horrid wanderings we had no familiarity, scarcely even that of speech. The
truth is that I was sickening for my grave, which is my best excuse. But besides that I was
of an unforgiving disposition from my birth, slow to take offence, slower to forget it, and
now incensed both against my companion and myself. For the best part of two days he was
unweariedly kind; silent, indeed, but always ready to help, and always hoping (as I could very
30   well see) that my displeasure would blow by. For the same length of time I stayed in myself,
nursing my anger, roughly refusing his services, and passing him over with my eyes as if he
had been a bush or a stone.

Questions

MARKS

21 Show how the writer's word choice in lines 1–8 emphasises how unpleasant
the journey is. Refer to **two** examples in your answer.   4

22 Show how the sentence structure in lines 9–19 helps to convey how David is
feeling. Refer to **two** examples in your answer.   4

23 Choose **one** example of the writer's use of language in lines 20–24 and explain
why you find it effective.   2

24 Look at lines 25–32. Describe in your own words the atmosphere between
David and Alan.   2

25 By referring to the extract and to elsewhere in the novel, show how David
suffers a number of physical hardships throughout the novel.   8

A

OR

Text 4 – Prose

If you choose this text you may not attempt a question on Prose in Section 2.
Read the extract below and then attempt the following questions.

The Telegram by Iain Crichton Smith

The extract is from the end of The Telegram.

'He has passed your house,' said the thin woman in a distant firm voice, and she looked up. He was walking along and he had indeed passed her house. She wanted to stand up and dance all round the kitchen, all fifteen stone of her, and shout and cry and sing a song but then she stopped. She couldn't do that. How could she do that when it must be the thin
5   woman's son? There was no other house. The thin woman was looking out at the elder, her lips pressed closely together, white and bloodless. Where had she learnt that self-control? She wasn't crying or shaking. She was looking out at something she had always dreaded but she wasn't going to cry or surrender or give herself away to anyone.

And at that moment the fat woman saw. She saw the years of discipline, she remembered
10   how thin and unfed and pale the thin woman had always looked, how sometimes she had had to borrow money, even a shilling to buy food. She saw what it must have been like to be a widow bringing up a son in a village not her own. She saw it so clearly that she was astounded. It was as if she had an extra vision, as if the air itself brought the past with all its details nearer. The number of times the thin woman had been ill and people had said that she
15   was weak and useless. She looked down at the thin woman's arm. It was so shrivelled, and dry.

And the elder walked on. A few yards now till he reached the plank. But the thin woman hadn't cried. She was steady and still, her lips still compressed, sitting upright in her chair. And, miracle of miracles, the elder passed the plank and walked straight on.

20   They looked at each other. What did it all mean? Where was the elder going, clutching his telegram in his hand, walking like a man in a daze? There were no other houses so where was he going? They drank their tea in silence, turning away from each other. The fat woman said, 'I must be going.' They parted for the moment without speaking. The thin woman still sat at the window looking out. Once or twice the fat woman made as if to turn back as if she
25   had something to say, some message to pass on, but she didn't. She walked away.

It wasn't till later that night that they discovered what had happened. The elder had a telegram directed to himself, to tell him of the drowning of his own son. He should never have seen it just like that, but there had been a mistake at the post office, owing to the fact that there were two boys in the village with the same name. His walk through the village was a
30   somnambulistic wandering. He didn't want to go home and tell his wife what had happened. He was walking along not knowing where he was going when later he was stopped half way to the next village. Perhaps he was going in search of his son. Altogether he had walked six miles. The telegram was crushed in his fingers and so sweaty that they could hardly make out the writing.

Questions

26 Look at lines 1–8. Explain briefly in your own words why the fat woman wanted 'to stand up and dance all round the kitchen', **and** why she did not do so.

2

27 'And at that moment the fat woman saw.' (line 9)

    a) By referring to lines 9–16, explain in your own words what it was she 'saw'.

2

    b) Explain how **two** examples of the writer's use of language in lines 9–16 emphasise the impact it has on the fat woman.

4

28 Explain **two** ways in which the language used in lines 20–25 creates a tense mood.

4

29 By referring to the extract and to at least one other story by Iain Crichton Smith, show how he ends his stories in a surprising or thought-provoking way.

8

OR

Text 5 – Prose

If you choose this text you may not attempt a question on Prose in Section 2.

Read the extract below and then attempt the following questions.

Virtual Pals by Anne Donovan

The extract is from Virtual Pals. *The opening sections of two consecutive messages between the girls are given below.*

```
e-mail
Date: 24.1.2001      2.43.34
From: sio2c@allan.gla.sch.uk
To: iri2c@allan.jupiter.net
```

5   Dear Irina,

Your e-mails are just pure brilliant. I don't know how you manage to write all they big words. I have to look up a dictionary to find the meanings of half of them. Miss Macintosh is dead chuffed cos she says it's gonnae improve my English. She really liked that bit about favourites.

10   Favourite just means the thing you like best, like your best TV programme or colour, you know, the one you'd pick if somebody gied you a choice. Maybe now you can tell me some of yours.

You know, Irina, I'm beginning to feel that you and me are real pals and that I can trust you. I do have pals here on earth but actually there's some things I can't talk to them about because

15   they might laugh at me or they might tell somebody else. So I'm gonnae to tell you because there's something about you that makes me feel you won't laugh at me, you take everything that serious, don't you? And anyway who could you tell? If you tellt your pals on Jupiter, well then it wouldn't matter if they laughed because they don't know me.

20 And now's a good time for me to explain it to you cos Miss Macintosh is off sick this week and the supply teacher that's takin us is no lookin at wer e-mails, he just tellt us to get on with our work and no disturb him. I think he's reading the paper actually but he's got it hidden inside a red folder ...

```
e-mail
Date: 25.1.2001   07.25.34.65
```
25 ```
From: iri2c@allan.jupiter.net
To: sio2c@allan.gla.sch.uk
```
Dear Siobhan,

I am delighted that you have trusted me with your confidences though I am somewhat concerned about their substance. From what you tell me about your feelings for this Paul
30 Wilson, it appears that they are very unhealthy. In last session's Applied Psychology module we dealt with the adolescent awakening of the sexual impulse. Believe me, it is not unusual for people of our age to project their emerging energies on to another being and to imagine all sorts of qualities which they do not in fact possess. Fantasising about this boy is a waste of time.

This is one of the reasons why in times past the female of the species tended to achieve less
35 than the male, as she was programmed biologically and sociologically to a more introspective and less active resolution of her sexuality. For many centuries we on Jupiter have undergone training programmes for both genders, designed to counteract these tendencies and promote greater equality.

# Questions

**MARKS**

**30** Why do you think the writer has included the information in lines 1–4 and lines 23–26? Give **two** reasons.

2

**31** Look at lines 6–12 and lines 28–33. By referring to at least one example from each message, show how the writer creates a contrast in the girls' language.

4

**32** Look at lines 13–22 and lines 34–38. Explain in your own words as far as possible what differences there are in the girls' level of maturity.

4

**33** Explain any **one** way in which these extracts are quite funny.

2

**34** *Virtual Pals* employs an unusual narrative technique. By referring to the extract and to at least one other story by Anne Donovan, show how the narrative technique helps to develop character and/or theme.

8
```

Section 1 – Scottish Text – 20 marks

Part C – Scottish Text – Poetry

Text 1 – Poetry

If you choose this text you may not attempt a question on Poetry in Section 2.
Read the poem below and then attempt the following questions.

Originally by Carol Ann Duffy

We came from our own country in a red room
which fell through the fields, our mother singing
our father's name to the turn of the wheels.
My brothers cried, one of them bawling *Home*,

5   *Home*, as the miles rushed back to the city,
the street, the house, the vacant rooms
where we didn't live any more. I stared
at the eyes of a blind toy, holding its paw.

All childhood is an emigration. Some are slow,

10   leaving you standing, resigned, up an avenue
where no one you know stays. Others are sudden.
Your accent wrong. Corners, which seem familiar,
leading to unimagined, pebble-dashed estates, big boys
eating worms and shouting words you don't understand.

15   My parents' anxiety stirred like a loose tooth
in my head. *I want our own country*, I said.

But then you forget, or don't recall, or change,
and, seeing your brother swallow a slug, feel only
a skelf of shame. I remember my tongue

20   shedding its skin like a snake, my voice
in the classroom sounding just like the rest. Do I only think
I lost a river, culture, speech, sense of first space
and the right place? Now, *Where do you come from?*
strangers ask. *Originally*? And I hesitate.

A

Questions

35 Summarise the key things that happen to the speaker of this poem. Make **four** points.

4

36 By referring to **two** examples from lines 9–14, show how the poet's use of language makes a clear distinction between 'slow' and 'sudden' emigration.

4

37 By referring to **two** examples from lines 17–24, show how the poet conveys the speaker's feelings of uncertainty.

4

38 By referring to this poem and to at least one other poem by Carol Ann Duffy, show how she creates a strong sense of character.

8

OR

Text 2 – Poetry

If you choose this text you may not attempt a question on Poetry in Section 2.
Read the extract below and then attempt the following questions.

In the Snack-bar by Edwin Morgan

The extract is from In the Snack-bar *(the last 29 lines).*

I press the pedal of the drier, draw his hands

gently into the roar of the hot air.

But he cannot rub them together,

drags out a handkerchief to finish.

5   He is glad to leave the contraption, and face the stairs.

He climbs, and steadily enough.

He climbs, we climb. He climbs

with many pauses but with that one

persisting patience of the undefeated

10   which is the nature of man when all is said.

And slowly we go up. And slowly we go up.

The faltering, unfaltering steps

take him at last to the door

across that endless, yet not endless waste of floor.

15   I watch him helped on a bus. It shudders off in the rain.

The conductor bends to hear where he wants to go.

Wherever he could go it would be dark

and yet he must trust men.

Without embarrassment or shame

20 he must announce his most pitiful needs

in a public place. No one sees his face.

Does he know how frightening he is in his strangeness

under his mountainous coat, his hands like wet leaves

stuck to the half-white stick?

25 His life depends on many who would evade him.

But he cannot reckon up the chances,

having one thing to do,

to haul his blind hump through these rains of August.

Dear Christ, to be born for this!

Questions

39 Summarise in your own words what happens in this part of the poem. Make at least **four** key points.

4

40 By referring to one example, show how the poet makes effective use of repetition in lines 6–11.

2

41 Look at lines 12–14. Explain what you think the poet means by **either** 'faltering, unfaltering' **or** 'endless, yet not endless'.

2

42 Show how **two** examples of the poet's use of language in lines 17–29 create sympathy for the old man.

4

43 By referring to 'In the Snack-bar' and at least one other poem by Edwin Morgan, show how he uses language effectively to describe a character **or** a place **or** an event.

8

OR

Text 3 – Poetry

If you choose this text you may not attempt a question on Poetry in Section 2.
Read the poem below and then attempt the following questions.

Assisi by Norman MacCaig

The dwarf with his hands on backwards

sat, slumped like a half-filled sack

on tiny twisted legs from which

sawdust might run,

5   outside the three tiers of churches built

in honour of St Francis, brother

of the poor, talker with birds, over whom

he had the advantage

of not being dead yet.

10   A priest explained

how clever it was of Giotto

to make his frescoes tell stories

that would reveal to the illiterate the goodness

of God and the suffering

15   of His Son. I understood

the explanation and

the cleverness.

A rush of tourists, clucking contentedly,

fluttered after him as he scattered

20   the grain of the Word. It was they who had passed

the ruined temple outside, whose eyes

wept pus, whose back was higher

than his head, whose lopsided mouth

said *Grazie* in a voice as sweet

25   as a child's when she speaks to her mother

or a bird's when it spoke

to St Francis.

Questions

MARKS

44 By referring to **two** examples of poetic techniques in lines 1–9, explain how the poet creates a vivid impression of the dwarf.

4

45 By referring to **two** examples of the poet's use of language in lines 18–20, explain how his contempt for the tourists is conveyed.

4

46 By referring to the poet's use of language in lines 20–27, show how he conveys contrasting impressions of the dwarf.

4

47 By referring to this poem and to at least one other poem by Norman MacCaig, show how he creates feelings of sympathy in the reader.

8

OR

Text 4 – Poetry

If you choose this text you may not attempt a question on Poetry in Section 2.
Read the extract below and then attempt the following questions.

Keeping Orchids by Jackie Kay

The extract is from Keeping Orchids *(the first 17 lines).*

The orchids my mother gave me when we first met
are still alive, twelve days later. Although

some of the buds remain closed as secrets.
Twice since I carried them back, like a baby in a shawl,

5   from her train station to mine, then home. Twice
since then the whole glass carafe has crashed

falling over, unprovoked, soaking my chest of drawers.
All the broken waters. I have rearranged

the upset orchids with troubled hands. Even after
10   that the closed ones did not open out. The skin

shut like an eye in the dark; the closed lid.
Twelve days later, my mother's hands are all I have.

Her face is fading fast. Even her voice rushes
through a tunnel the other way from home.

15   I close my eyes and try to remember exactly:
a paisley pattern scarf, a brooch, a navy coat.

A digital watch her daughter was wearing when she died.

Questions

48 Look at lines 1–11.

   a) Using your own words as far as possible, identify **four** ways in which the speaker's behaviour makes it clear that the orchids are important to her.   4

   b) Show how the poet's language conveys the idea that the orchids are a little mysterious. Refer to **two** examples in your answer.   4

49 By referring to lines 12–17, show how the poet's language emphasises the difficulty the speaker has remembering her mother. Refer to **two** examples in your answer.   4

50 Jackie Kay's poems often feature characters who are lonely or isolated or frustrated. By referring to *Keeping Orchids* and to at least one other poem by Jackie Kay, show how she explores one of these ideas.   8

[End of section 1]

Section 2 – Critical Essay – 20 marks

Attempt **ONE** question from the following genres – Drama, Prose, Poetry, Film and Television Drama, or Language.

Your answer must be on a different genre from that chosen in Section 1.

You should spend approximately 45 minutes on this Section.

Drama

Answers to questions on Drama should refer to the text and to such relevant features as characterisation, key scene(s), structure, climax, theme, plot, conflict, setting ...

1   Choose a play in which there is a character who suffers from a human weakness such as jealousy, pride, ambition, selfishness, lust.
By referring to appropriate techniques, show how the weakness is revealed, and then explain how this weakness affects both the characters and the events of the play.

2   Choose a scene from a play in which suspense or tension is built up.
By referring to appropriate techniques, show how this suspense or tension is built up and what effect this scene has on the play as a whole.

Prose

Answers to questions on Prose should refer to the text and to such relevant features as characterisation, setting, language, key incident(s), climax, turning point, plot, structure, narrative technique, theme, ideas, description ...

3   Choose a novel **or** short story in which there is a character you admire or dislike or feel sorry for.
By referring to appropriate techniques, show how the author creates this character, and say why you feel this way about him/her.

4   Choose a novel **or** a short story **or** a work of non-fiction which explores a theme which you think is important.
By referring to appropriate techniques, show how the author explores this theme.

Poetry

Answers to questions on Poetry should refer to the text and to such relevant features as word choice, tone, imagery, structure, content, rhythm, rhyme, theme, sound, ideas ...

5   Choose a poem which presents a memorable picture of a person or of a place.
By referring to poetic techniques, explain how the poet makes the picture memorable.

6   Choose a poem which made you think more deeply about an aspect of life you think is important.
By referring to poetic techniques, show how the poet explores this aspect of life.

Film and Television Drama

Answers to questions on Film and Television Drama should refer to the text and to such relevant features as use of camera, key sequence, characterisation, mise-en-scène, editing, setting, music/sound, special effects, plot, dialogue ...

7 Choose a scene or sequence from a film **or** television drama* in which tension is created.
By referring to appropriate techniques, explain how the tension is created.

8 Choose a film **or** television drama* which has a character who can be described as a hero or as a villain or as a mixture of both.
By referring to appropriate techniques, explain how the character is presented in the film or television drama.*

  * 'television drama' includes a single play, a series or a serial.

Language

Answers to questions on Language should refer to the text and to such relevant features as register, accent, dialect, slang, jargon, vocabulary, tone, abbreviation ...

9 Choose a text which you consider to be persuasive, for example an advertisement or a speech or a newspaper column.
By referring to specific examples, explain how successful the persuasive language is.

10 Consider the specialist language used by a group of people to talk about a particular topic, for example a sport or a job or a hobby or a pastime.
By referring to specific examples and to appropriate techniques, explain how the specialist language used by the group is effective in communicating ideas clearly.

[End of section 2]

[End of question paper]

National 5 English

HODDER
GIBSON
LEARN MORE

Paper 1: Reading for Understanding, Analysis and Evaluation

Duration: 1 hour

Total marks: 30

Attempt ALL questions.

Write your answers clearly in the answer booklet provided. In the answer booklet you must clearly identify the question number you are attempting.

Use **blue** or **black** ink.

Before leaving the examination room you must give your answer booklet to the Invigilator; if you do not you may lose all the marks for this paper.

The real price of gold

Like many of his Inca ancestors, Juan Apaza is possessed by gold. Descending into an icy tunnel 17,000 feet up in the Peruvian Andes, the 44-year-old miner stuffs a wad of coca leaves into his mouth to brace himself for the inevitable hunger and fatigue. For 30 days each month Apaza toils, without pay, deep inside this mine dug down under a glacier above the
5   world's highest town, La Rinconada. For 30 days he faces the dangers that have killed many of his fellow miners – explosives, toxic gases, tunnel collapses – to extract the gold that the world demands. Apaza does all this, without pay, so that he can make it to today, the 31st day, when he and his fellow miners are given a single shift, four hours or maybe a little more, to haul out and keep as much rock as their weary shoulders can bear. Under the ancient system
10 that still prevails in the high Andes, this is what passes for a pay cheque: a sack of rocks that may contain a small fortune in gold or, far more often, very little at all.

For more than 500 years the glittering seams trapped beneath the glacial ice here, three miles above sea level, have drawn people to this place in Peru. First the Inca, then the Spanish, whose lust for gold and silver spurred the conquest of the New World. But it is only
15 now, as the price of gold soars – it has risen 235 percent in the past eight years – that 30,000 people have flocked to La Rinconada, turning a lonely prospectors' camp into a squalid shantytown on top of the world. Fuelled by luck and desperation, sinking in its own toxic waste and lawlessness, this no-man's-land now teems with dreamers and schemers anxious to strike it rich, even if it means destroying their environment – and themselves – in the
20 process.

Only gold, that object of desire and destruction, could have conjured up a place of such startling contradictions as La Rinconada. Remote and inhospitable – at 17,000 feet, even oxygen is in short supply – the town is, nevertheless, growing at a furious pace. Approaching the settlement from across the high plains, a visitor first sees the glint of rooftops under a
25 magnificent glacier draped like a wedding veil across the mountain. Then comes the stench.

It's not just the garbage dumped down the slope, but the human and industrial waste that clogs the settlement's streets.

The scene may sound almost medieval, but La Rinconada is one of the frontiers of a thoroughly modern phenomenon: a 21st-century gold rush.

30 No single element has tantalized and tormented the human imagination more than the shimmering metal known by the chemical symbol *Au*. For thousands of years the desire to possess gold has driven people to extremes, fuelling wars and conquests, underpinning empires and currencies, levelling mountains and forests. Gold is not vital to human existence; it has, in fact, relatively few practical uses. Yet its chief virtues – its unusual density and

35 its imperishable shine – have made it one of the world's most coveted commodities, a transcendent symbol of beauty, wealth, and immortality. From pharaohs (who insisted on being buried in what they called the 'flesh of the gods') to the forty-niners (whose mad rush for the mother lode built the American West) to the financiers (who made it the bedrock of the global economy): nearly every society through the ages has invested gold with an almost

40 mythological power.

For all of its allure, gold's human and environmental toll has never been so steep. Part of the challenge, as well as the fascination, is that there is so little of it. In all of history, only 161,000 tons of gold have been mined, barely enough to fill two Olympic-size swimming pools. More than half of that has been extracted in the past 50 years. Now the world's richest

45 deposits are fast being depleted, and new discoveries are rare. Gone are the hundred-mile-long gold reefs in South Africa or cherry-size nuggets in California. Most of the gold left to mine exists as traces buried in remote and fragile corners of the globe. It's an invitation to destruction. But there is no shortage of miners, big and small, who are willing to accept.

At one end of the spectrum are the armies of poor migrant workers converging on small-

50 scale mines like La Rinconada. Employing crude methods that have hardly changed in centuries, they produce about 25 percent of the world's gold. At the other end of the spectrum are vast, open-pit mines run by the world's largest mining companies. Using armadas of supersize machines, these big-footprint mines produce three-quarters of the world's gold.

Gold mining, however, generates more waste per ounce than any other metal, and the mines'

55 mind-bending disparities of scale show why: these gashes in the Earth are so massive they can be seen from space, yet the particles being mined in them are so microscopic that, in many cases, more than 200 could fit on the head of a pin. There is no avoiding the brutal calculus of gold mining: extracting a single ounce of gold – the amount in a typical wedding ring – requires the removal of more than 250 tons of rock and ore.

60 Back in La Rinconada, Apaza is still waiting for a stroke of luck. 'Maybe today will be the big one,' he says. To improve his odds, the miner has already made his 'payment to the Earth': a bottle of pisco, the local liquor, placed near the mouth of the mine; a few coca leaves slipped under a rock; and, several months back, a rooster sacrificed on the sacred mountaintop. Now, heading into the tunnel, he mumbles a prayer in his native Quechua language to the deity who

65 rules the mountain and all the gold within.

Brook Larmer, in National Geographic *magazine (adapted)*

Questions

MARKS

1   Look at lines 1–11, and then explain **in your own words four** things that make
    Juan Apaza's working life harsh.

    4

2   Look at lines 12–20, and then explain how **two** examples of the writer's **word
    choice** demonstrate how unpleasant La Rinconada has become.

    4

3   Look at lines 21–27, and then explain how the language used demonstrates
    that La Rinconada is 'a place of ... contradictions'.

    4

4   Explain why the sentence 'The scene ... gold rush' (lines 28–29) provides an
    appropriate link at this point in the passage.

    2

5   Look at lines 30–40, and then summarise, **using your own words** as far as
    possible, some of the points made about gold. You should make **five** key points
    in your answer.

    5

6   Look at lines 41–48, and then explain **in your own words** why it is difficult to
    mine gold today.

    3

7   Look at lines 49–53, and then explain how **two** examples of the language used
    demonstrate the destructive nature of gold mining.

    4

8   Look at lines 54–59, and then explain **in your own words** what the writer
    means by 'disparities of scale'.

    2

9   Explain why the last paragraph (lines 60–65) provides an effective conclusion to
    the passage as a whole.

    2

[End of question paper]

Paper 2: Critical Reading

Duration: 90 minutes

Total marks – 40

SECTION 1 – Scottish Text – 20 marks

Read an extract from a Scottish text you have previously studied.

Choose ONE text from either

Part A – Drama   Pages 33—37

or

Part B – Prose   Pages 38—45

or

Part C – Poetry   Pages 46—50

Attempt ALL the questions for your chosen text.

SECTION 2 – Critical Essay – 20 marks

Attempt ONE question from the following genres – Drama, Prose, Poetry, Film and Television Drama, or Language.

Your answer must be on a different genre from that chosen in Section 1.

You should spend approximately 45 minutes on each Section.

Write your answers clearly in the answer booklet provided. In the answer booklet you must clearly identify the question number you are attempting.

Use **blue** or **black** ink.

Before leaving the examination room you must give your answer booklet to the Invigilator; if you do not you may lose all the marks for this paper.

Section 1 – Scottish Text – 20 marks

Part A – Scottish Text – Drama

Text 1 – Drama

If you choose this text you may not attempt a question on Drama in Section 2.
Read the extract below and then attempt the following questions.

Bold Girls by Rona Munro

The extract is from Scene One. Deirdre appears in Marie's house for the first time.

Deirdre comes into the room. She stands uncertain in the centre of the room.
Marie enters behind her.

The three older women just stare at Deirdre
DEIRDRE: Can I stay here till I'm dry, Mrs? They won't let me up the road.

5   *There is a pause then Marie finally stirs*
MARIE: You better sit down by the fire (*She switches on the TV*)

Deirdre sits by the fire
Nora, Marie and Cassie slowly sit as well, watching her
NORA: I don't know your face.

10   *Deirdre says nothing. She doesn't look up from the fire*
      Well where are you from?
Deirdre jerks her head without turning
      Where?
DEIRDRE: (*sullen, quietly*) Back of the school there.
15   NORA: What's that?
     DEIRDRE: (*loudly*) Back of the school there.
     NORA: Those houses next the off-licence?
Deirdre nods
      I know where you are. So what happened to you then?
20   *Deirdre shrugs. She looks up and catches Cassie's eye*
Cassie turns quickly to look at the TV
MARIE: Will you take a cup of tea, love?
Deirdre nods
Marie goes to make it
25   *Nora stares at Deirdre a while longer, then turns to Cassie*
     NORA: So Cassie, looks like that wee brother of yours will miss his tea altogether?

	CASSIE:	*(with her eyes on the TV)* Looks like he might.
	NORA:	I hope he's the sense to stay in town.
30	CASSIE:	Sure he'll phone next door, let us know what's happening.
	NORA:	Aye he's a good boy.

There is a pause while everyone watches the TV in an uncomfortable silence

Marie brings Deirdre the tea and some biscuits. Deirdre takes it without saying anything,
starts to eat and drink furtively and ravenously. Cassie and Marie exchange glances over
35 *her head*

	MARIE:	Turn the sound up on that will you, Nora?

Questions

MARKS

1 By referring to the whole extract, identify **four** ways in which Deirdre's behaviour makes her appear strange.

4

2 Describe the way each of the three older women treats Deirdre. Support your answers with reference to the text.

6

3 Why do you think Marie asks Nora to turn up the sound on the TV? (line 36)

2

4 By referring to this extract and to the play as a whole, show how the role of Deirdre is important in the play.

8

OR

Text 2 – Drama

If you choose this text you may not attempt a question on Drama in Section 2.
Read the extract below and then attempt the following questions.

Sailmaker by Alan Spence

The extract is from Act One. Davie and Billy discuss money problems.

(Enter DAVIE *and* BILLY, *talking as they walk)*

	DAVIE:	Eh, Billy … that coupla quid ah tapped off ye. Could it wait till next week?
	BILLY:	Aye sure.
	DAVIE:	Things are still a wee bit tight.
5	BILLY:	What's the score?
	DAVIE:	Eh?
	BILLY:	Ye shouldnae be this skint. What is it?
	DAVIE:	Ah told ye. It's the job. Just hasnae been so great. No sellin enough. No collectin enough. No gettin much over the basic.

10	BILLY:	Aye, but ye should be able tae get by. Just the two ae ye.
	DAVIE:	It's no easy.
	BILLY:	Ye bevvyin?
	DAVIE:	Just a wee half when ah finish ma work. An by Christ ah need it.
	BILLY:	Ye bettin too heavy? Is that it?
15	DAVIE:	(*Hesitates then decides to tell him*) It started a coupla months ago. Backed a favourite. Absolute surefire certainty. Couldnae lose. But it was even money, so ah had tae put quite a whack on it. (*Slightly shamefaced*) Best part ae a week's wages.
	BILLY:	An it got beat?
20	DAVIE:	Out the park. So ah made it up by borrowin off the bookie. He does his moneylender on the side. Charges interest.
	BILLY:	An every week ye miss the interest goes up.
	DAVIE:	This is it. Now when ah pay him ah'm just clearin the interest. Ah'm no even touchin the original amount ah borrowed. Ah must've paid him back
25		two or three times over, an ah still owe him the full whack.
	BILLY:	Bastard, eh? Sicken ye. *And* he's a pape.
	(DAVIE *laughs*)	
	DAVIE:	Still, Aw ah need's a wee turn. Ah mean ma luck's got tae change sometime hasn't it? Law of averages.
30	BILLY:	Whatever that is.
	DAVIE:	Things have got tae get better.
	BILLY:	It's a mug's game. The punter canny win.
	DAVIE:	Got tae keep tryin.
	BILLY:	Flingin it away!
35		Look, Don't get me wrong. Ah don't mind helpin ye out, but ah'm no exactly rollin in it maself.
	DAVIE:	You'll get yer money back.
	BILLY:	That's no what ah mean!
	DAVIE:	What am ah supposed tae dae? Get a job as a company director or
40		somethin! Ah'll go doon tae the broo in the mornin!
	BILLY:	There must be some way tae get this bookie aff yer back for a start.
	DAVIE:	Aye sure!
	BILLY:	Ah mean, you've *paid* him.
	DAVIE:	Ah knew his terms.
45	BILLY:	It's no even legal.
	DAVIE:	Neither is gettin his heavies tae kick folk's heids in.
	BILLY:	So maybe he's no the only wan that knows a few hard men.
	DAVIE:	(*Sighs*) What a carry on, eh?

Questions

MARKS

5 By referring to the whole extract, explain why Davie is having money problems. Make at least **four** key points.

4

6 What **two** things do we learn about Billy in lines 1–14?

2

7 Why do you think Davie laughs (line 27)? Give **two** reasons.

2

8 Look at lines 28–48. By referring closely to the text, explain how the dialogue in these lines shows clearly the difference in outlook between Davie and Billy.

4

9 Money problems and ways to escape them are an important theme in *Sailmaker*. With close reference to the extract and elsewhere in the play, show how this theme is explored.

8

OR

Text 3 – Drama

If you choose this text you may not attempt a question on Drama in Section 2.

Read the extract below and then attempt the following questions.

Tally's Blood by Ann Marie Di Mambro

The extract is from Act Two, Scene Two. Rosinella tries to encourage Lucia's interest in Italian men.

	ROSINELLA:	You'll need to let your Uncle Massimo see the way you do the jiving, Lucia. She looks lovely so she does. Her hair swinging about her face. You get to see her lovely legs when she birrels about. And her eyes are all lit up and she's smiling. I wish Silvio Palombo could see you. How come you never danced that way with him at the Ice Cream dance, eh? Too shy, eh? … You like Silvio Palombo, don't you?
5		
	LUCIA:	He's OK.
	ROSINELLA:	Nice-looking boy too.
	LUCIA:	He's OK.
10	ROSINELLA:	Oh come on, Lucia, you can't kid me on. I know you're daft for him. But I like the way you kind of stand back a bit, don't let him see you're keen. Italian boys like that.
	LUCIA:	Auntie Rosinella …?
	ROSINELLA:	He cannie keep his eyes off you. And if he's who you want, then it's not for me to stand in your way. But I told his mother. I made sure I told her. 'Mrs Palombo,' I said, 'our Lucia's a lady, she's not been brought up to work in a shop, running after some man.' I tell you, Lucia, she liked me for that. They've got class, that family.
15		

	LUCIA:	Auntie Rosinella ...?
20	ROSINELLA:	I hear them all the time. 'Ma lassie's an awfy good worker' – 'Ma lassie cleaned four chickens' – I promised myself, my Lucia's to marry a man that really loves HER – no to put her in a shop and make her work. How much you got there?
	LUCIA:	Three pounds, seven and tenpence ha'penny.
25	ROSINELLA:	That's what I want for you – a good life, with a good Italian man – here.
	LUCIA:	Auntie Rosinella.
	ROSINELLA:	You see the way the Italians are getting on now, eh? Beginning to make a wee bit money? Because they're prepared to WORK, that's why. I don't know anybody works so hard as the Italian men.
30	*Hughie in: with pail and mop.*	
	HUGHIE:	That's the tables cleared and the front shop mopped, Mrs Pedreschi, and the chip pan cleaned out. Is the milk boiled?
	ROSINELLA:	Should be.

She turns attention back to Lucia, Hughie lifts pot from stove and pours contents into two pails: he
35 *covers them and sets them aside, working like a Trojan.*

	ROSINELLA:	And the way they love their families. Nobody loves their families like the Italians. You want to stay for a wee bit pasta, Hughie? It's your favourite. Rigatoni.
	HUGHIE:	No thanks, Mrs Pedreschi. I better get up the road. Bridget's going out and
40		I don't like my mammy left on her own.

Questions

MARKS

10 Show how the playwright makes you aware of **two** aspects of Rosinella's character in lines 1–25.

4

11 Look at lines 27–40.

a) Identify the **two** things that Rosinella admires about Italians and show how her use of language makes her admiration clear.

4

b) Explain how Hughie's words and/or actions suggest that Rosinella is being prejudiced.

4

12 By referring to the extract and to elsewhere in the play, show how the theme of prejudice is explored.

8

Section 1 – Scottish Text – 20 marks

Part B – Scottish Text – Prose

Text 1 – Prose

If you choose this text you may not attempt a question on Prose in Section 2.

Read the extract below and then attempt the following questions.

The Cone-Gatherers by Robin Jenkins

The extract is from Chapter 11. Calum and Neil are in a tree when a storm begins and they climb down to seek shelter.

The brothers crept slowly downward. Every time lightning flashed and thunder crashed they thought their tree had been shattered, and clung, helpless as woodlice, waiting to be hurled to the ground with the fragments. The tree itself seemed to be terrified; every branch, every twig, heaved and slithered. At times it seemed to have torn its roots in its terror and to be
5 dangling in the air.

At last they reached the ground. At once Neil flung his bag of cones down and snatched up his knapsack. He shouted to Calum to do likewise.

'We'd never get to the hut alive,' he gasped. 'We'd get killed among the trees. Forby, it's too far away. We're going to the beach hut.'

10 'But we're not allowed, Neil.'

Neil clutched his brother and spoke to him as calmly as he could.

'I ken it's not allowed, Calum,' he said. 'I ken we gave our promise to Mr. Tulloch not to get into any more trouble. But look at the rain. We're soaked already. I've got rheumatics, and you ken your chest is weak. If we shelter under a tree it might get struck by lightning and we'd be
15 killed. In three minutes we can reach the beach hut.'

'But we promised, Neil. The lady will be angry again.'

'Do you want me then to be a useless cripple for the rest of my days? What if she is angry? All she can do is to tell us to leave her wood, and I'll be glad to go. I don't want you to do what you think is wrong, Calum; but sometimes we've got to choose between two things, neither of
20 them to our liking. We'll do no harm. We'll leave the place as we find it. Nobody will ever ken we've been in it. What do you say then?'

Calum nodded unhappily.

'I think maybe we should go,' he said.

'All right then. We'd better run for it. But didn't I tell you to drop your cone bag?'

25 'They'll get all wet, Neil.'

Neil stood gaping; he saw the rain streaming down the green grime on his brother's face; beyond Calum was the wood shrouded in wet.

'They'll get wet,' he heard himself repeating.

'Aye, that's right, Neil. Mind what Mr. Tulloch said, if they get wet they're spoiled.'

30 It was no use being bitter or angry or sarcastic.

'Is there never to be any sun again then,' cried Neil, 'to dry them?'

Calum looked up at the sky.

'I think so, Neil,' he murmured.

Questions

MARKS

13 Explain **two** ways in which the writer's use of language in lines 1–5 conveys the violence of the storm.

> 4

14 Look at lines 6–10. Show how **one** example of the writer's word choice makes clear how impatient Neil is.

> 2

15 Using your own words as far as possible, summarise the key points in Neil's argument to persuade Calum to go to the beach hut (lines 12–21). Make at least **four** key points.

> 4

16 Explain how the writer makes Calum seem childlike in lines 25–33.

> 2

17 By referring to this extract and to elsewhere in the novel, show how the relationship between Calum and Neil is developed.

> 8

OR

Text 2 – Prose

If you choose this text you may not attempt a question on Prose in Section 2.

Read the extract below and then attempt the following questions.

The Testament of Gideon Mack by James Robertson

The extract is from Chapter 7. It is Sunday, and Gideon is watching television when he hears his father's voice.

Another few minutes must have gone by. I forgot where I was and what day it was. The sound was louder than I'd intended. I was only a foot away from the screen, finger hovering near the off switch, and maybe that was why I failed to hear my father's footsteps in the hall. By the time the door opened and his voice filled the room – 'Agnes? I thought
5   I heard somebody …' – there was no point in even bothering to switch the television off. I did, though, and jumped to my feet in a flush of shame and fury.

He closed the door behind him. I stood between him and the television set as if to protect it, as if to say it was not to blame. I could see the wee flames in his cheeks. I bowed my head, fixing my eye on a crack in the skirting board. I heard him say, 'Put it back on.'

10 'No, no, it doesn't matter, I'm sorry,' I mumbled. Entirely the wrong thing. He cut me off, his voice shaking.

'It doesn't *matter*?' he said. 'Do you dare to disobey me? Put it back on.'

I turned and reached for the switch. The television, being warm, came on at once. If my father understood that, he made no allowance for it.

15 'I see you have become very skilled at operating that thing,' he said quietly, almost admiringly. 'How often have you done this?'

'Never,' I said. It was true that I'd not touched the set before on a Sunday. 'I promise, this is the first time.'

'It will be the last,' he said. 'Come here.'

20 He pointed beside him and I went and stood there. His huge right hand descended on my neck and the thumb and fingers gripped it so that I cried out. He increased the pressure. I thought my head would snap off. His breathing was like that of some monstrous creature in its den. The blood in his fingers pulsed furiously against my neck.

Thus we stood in front of the television together, father and son, for the remaining ten
25 minutes of the programme. It felt like an hour. If I squirmed to try and ease the pain, his grip tightened. I hated him then, hated what he was doing to me and hated my own helplessness. *ZAP! BLAM! POW!* I hated the screen with its cartoon punches and I hated the way the parlour echoed with screeching tyres and wisecracks delivered in American accents. I saw it as if through his eyes – cheap, tawdry, meaningless rubbish – and I longed for it to end.

30 He pushed me from him as the credits rolled and the inane theme music played. 'Turn it off,' he said. I did as I was told, rubbing my neck and wiping away the tears that he had squeezed out of me.

'What ... is ... that?' he said, dropping the words methodically into the silence.

'*Batman*,' I said.

35 'Bat ... man,' he said.

'Yes,' I said. And then again, 'I'm sorry.' But I don't think he heard that.

'It is not bat ... man,' he said, and I could not stop myself, I was trying to explain, I said, 'It *is*.'

'Do not interrupt me,' he said. His voice grew louder and harder. 'Do not contradict me. It is not bat ... man, whatever that means. I'll tell you what it is. It is drivel. It is the most
40 unutterable garbage I have ever witnessed. Garbage from the land of garbage.'

Questions

MARKS

18 Look at lines 1–11 and explain how the writer makes you aware of Gideon's nervousness when he hears his father. Refer to **two** examples.

4

19 Show how **two** examples of the language used in lines 12–32 convey the aggressiveness of Gideon's father.

4

20 Show how **two** examples of the language used in lines 33–40 convey the father's contempt for American culture.

4

21 By referring to the extract and to elsewhere in the novel, show how the relationship between Gideon and his father is portrayed.

8

OR

Text 3 – Prose

If you choose this text you may not attempt a question on Prose in Section 2.

Read the extract below and then attempt the following questions.

Kidnapped by Robert Louis Stevenson

The extract is from Chapter 19 – The House of Fear. *David and Alan arrive at the home of James Stewart of the Glens.*

At last, about half-past ten of the clock, we came to the top of a brae, and saw lights below us. It seemed a house door stood open and let out a beam of fire and candle-light; and all round the house and steading five or six persons were moving hurriedly about, each carrying a lighted brand.

5 'James must have tint his wits,' said Alan. 'If this was the soldiers instead of you and me, he would be in a bonny mess. But I dare say he'll have a sentry on the road, and he would ken well enough no soldiers would find the way that we came.'

Hereupon he whistled three times, in a particular manner. It was strange to see how, at the first sound of it, all the moving torches came to a stand, as if the bearers were 10 affrighted; and how, at the third, the bustle began again as before.

Having thus set folks' minds at rest, we came down the brae, and were met at the yard gate (for this place was like a well-doing farm) by a tall, handsome man of more than fifty, who cried out to Alan in the Gaelic.

'James Stewart,' said Alan, 'I will ask ye to speak in Scotch, for here is a young gentleman 15 with me that has nane of the other. This is him,' he added, putting his arm through mine, 'a young gentleman of the Lowlands, and a laird in his country too, but I am thinking it will be the better for his health if we give his name the go-by.'

James of the Glens turned to me for a moment, and greeted me courteously enough; the next he had turned to Alan.

20 'This has been a dreadful accident,' he cried. 'It will bring trouble on the country.' And he wrung his hands.

'Hoots!' said Alan, 'ye must take the sour with the sweet, man. Colin Roy is dead, and be thankful for that!'

'Ay,' said James, 'and by my troth, I wish he was alive again! It's all very fine to blow and boast
25 beforehand; but now it's done, Alan; and who's to bear the wyte of it? The accident fell out in Appin – mind ye that, Alan; it's Appin that must pay; and I am a man that has a family.'

While this was going on I looked about me at the servants. Some were on ladders, digging in the thatch of the house or the farm buildings, from which they brought out guns, swords, and different weapons of war; others carried them away; and by the sound of mattock blows from
30 somewhere farther down the brae, I suppose they buried them. Though they were all so busy, there prevailed no kind of order in their efforts; men struggled together for the same gun and ran into each other with their burning torches; and James was continually turning about from his talk with Alan, to cry out orders which were apparently never understood. The faces in the torchlight were like those of people overborne with hurry and panic; and though none spoke
35 above his breath, their speech sounded both anxious and angry.

Questions

MARKS

22 By referring to lines 1–7, give **two** reasons why Alan thinks that 'James must have tint his wits'.

2

23 By referring to lines 14–17, explain what impression Alan is trying to create of David when he introduces him to James Stewart.

2

24 By referring to lines 20–26, explain in your own words the differing reactions of Alan and James to the 'accident'.

4

25 Explain how the language used in lines 27–35 creates an atmosphere of panic. You should refer to **two** examples.

4

26 By referring to the extract and to elsewhere in the novel, show how the writer presents the character of Alan Breck.

8

OR

Text 4 – Prose

If you choose this text you may not attempt a question on Prose in Section 2.

Read the extract below and then attempt the following questions.

Mother and Son by Iain Crichton Smith

The extract is from near the beginning of Mother and Son.

In the bed was a woman. She was sleeping, her mouth tightly shut and prim and anaemic. There was a bitter smile on her lips as if fixed there; just as you sometimes see the

insurance man coming to the door with the same smile each day, the same brilliant smile which never falls away till he's gone into the anonymity of the streets. The forehead was not
5   very high and not low, though its wrinkles gave it an expression of concentration as if the woman were wrestling with some terrible witch's idea in dreams.

The man looked at her for a moment, then fumbled for his matches again and began to light a fire. The sticks fell out of place and he cursed vindictively and helplessly. For a moment he sat squatting on his haunches staring into the fire, as if he were thinking of some state of
10   innocence, some state to which he could not return: a reminiscent smile dimpled his cheeks and showed in eyes which immediately became still and dangerous again.

The clock struck five wheezingly and, at the first chime, the woman woke up. She started as she saw the figure crouched over the fire and then subsided: 'It's only you.' There was relief in the voice, but there was a curious hint of contempt or acceptance. He still sat staring into the
15   fire and answered dully: 'Yes, it's only me!' He couldn't be said to speak the words: they fell away from him as sometimes happens when one is in a deep reverie where every question is met by its answer almost instinctively.

'Well, what's the matter with you!' she snapped pettishly, 'sitting there moping with the tea to be made. I sometimes don't know why we christened you John' – with a sigh. 'My father was
20   never like you. He was a man who knew his business.'

'All right, *all* right,' he said despairingly. 'Can't you get a new record for your gramophone. I've heard all that before,' as if he were conscious of the inadequacy of this familiar retort – he added: 'hundreds of times.' But she wasn't to be stopped.

'I can't understand what has come over you lately. You keep mooning about the house, pacing
25   up and down with your hands in your pockets. Do you know what's going to happen to you, you'll be taken to the asylum. That's where you'll go. Your father's people had something wrong with their heads, it was in your family but not in ours.'

Questions

27 Explain **two** ways the language used in lines 1–6 creates an unpleasant impression of the mother.

4

28 By referring to the language used in lines 7–17, explain **two** impressions you are given of the son's character.

4

29 Show how the language used in lines 18–27 conveys the hostile atmosphere between mother and son. Refer to **two** examples in your answer.

4

30 By referring to the extract and to at least one other story by Crichton Smith, show how he explores conflict between characters.

8

B

OR

Text 5 – Prose

If you choose this text you may not attempt a question on Prose in Section 2.

Read the extract below and then attempt the following questions.

Away in a Manger by Anne Donovan

The extract is from Away in a Manger.

They turned the corner and the cauld evaporated. The square shimmerin wi light, brightness sharp against the gloomy street. Trees frosted wi light. Lights shaped intae circles and flowers, like the plastic jewellery sets wee lassies love. Lights switchin on and off in a mad rhythm ae their ain, tryin tae look like bells ringin and snow fallin. Reindeer

5 and Santas, holly, ivy, robins, all bleezin wi light. Amy gazed at them, eyes shinin.

'Haud ma haund tight tae we get across this road. There's lots of motors here.' Sandra pulled Amy close in tae her. 'They're lovely, aren't they?'

'Uh huh.' Amy nodded. 'Can we walk right round the square?'

A tape of Christmas carols was playin on the sound system, fillin the air like a cracklin

10 heavenly choir. Sandra and Amy joined the other faimlies wanderin round.

'Look at they reindeer, Mark!'

'There's a star, Daddy!'

'Check the size a that tree!'

Amy stopped in front of the big Christmas tree in the centre of the square.

15 'Can we sit doon tae look at it, Mammy?'

'Naw, just keep walkin, pet. It's too cauld.'

Anyway, nearly every bench was occupied. Newspapers neatly smoothed oot like bedclothes. Some folk were huddled under auld coats, tryin tae sleep their way intae oblivion while others sat upright, hauf-empty cans in their haunds, starin at the passers-

20 by. Sandra minded when she was wee and her mammy'd brought her tae see the lights. There were folk on the benches then, down-and-outs, faces shrunk wi drink and neglect, an auld cap lyin hauf-heartedly by their sides. But now the people who slept in the square werenae just auld drunks and it was hard tae pick them oot fae everyone else. That couple ower there wi their bags roond them, were they just havin a rest fae their Christmas

25 shoppin, watchin the lights? But who in their right minds would be sittin on a bench in George Square on this freezin cauld night if they'd a hame tae go tae?

Amy tugged at her airm. 'Ah know that song.'

'Whit song?'

'That one.' Amy pointed upwards. 'Silent Night, Holy Night.'

30 'Do you?'

'We learned it at school. Mrs Anderson was tellin us aboot the baby Jesus and how there was nae room at the inn so he was born in a stable.'

'Oh.'

'It's no ma favourite, but.'

35 'What's no your favourite?'

'Silent Night. Guess what ma favourite is?'

'Don't know.'

'Guess, Mammy, you have tae guess.'

Sandra couldnae be bothered guessin but she knew there'd be nae peace tae she'd made
40 some attempt and anyway, Amy'd get bored wi the 'Guess what?' game quick enough.

'Little donkey?'

'Naw.'

'O Little Town of Bethlehem?'

'Naw. Gie in?'

45 'OK.'

'Away in a Manger. Ah've won!' Amy jumped up and doon. 'Mammy, what's a manger?'

Questions

MARKS

31 Look at lines 1–13. By referring to **two** examples, explain how the writer's
language creates a mood of excitement.

4

32 Look at lines 17–26. Show how the writer's language conveys a vivid impression
of people on the benches

  a) Show how **one** example of the writer's language conveys a vivid impression
of the people on the benches **now**.

2

  b) Show how **one** example of the writer's language conveys a vivid impression
of the people on the benches **in the past**.

2

33 Look at the conversation between Sandra and her daughter in lines 27–46.
By referring closely to the text, identify **four** ways in which the conversation is
typical of one between an excited child and a parent.

4

34 By referring to the extract and to at least one other story by Anne Donovan,
show how the theme of parent/child relationships is developed.

8

Section 1 – Scottish Text – 20 marks

Part C – Scottish Text – Poetry

Text 1 – Poetry

If you choose this text you may not attempt a question on Poetry in Section 2.
Read the poem below and then attempt the following questions.

Anne Hathaway by Carol Ann Duffy

The bed we loved in was a spinning world
of forests, castles, torchlight, clifftops, seas
where he would dive for pearls. My lover's words
were shooting stars which fell to earth as kisses

5   on these lips; my body now a softer rhyme
to his, now echo, assonance; his touch
a verb dancing in the centre of a noun.
Some nights, I dreamed he'd written me, the bed
a page beneath his writer's hands. Romance

10   and drama played by touch, by scent, by taste.
In the other bed, the best, our guests dozed on,
dribbling their prose. My living laughing love –
I hold him in the casket of my widow's head
as he held me upon that next best bed.

Questions

MARKS

35 By referring to **two** examples of the poet's use of language in the first sentence of the poem ('The bed ... pearls.'), show how a sense of joy and happiness is conveyed.

4

36 In the next two sentences of the poem ('My lover's words ... writer's hands.'), there are many references to writing poetry and plays. Choose any **two** examples of this and explain in detail how each one adds to your understanding of the speaker's feelings.

4

37 Show how, in lines 11–14, the poet's language makes clear how different the guests are from the speaker and her lover. Refer to **two** examples in your answer.

4

38 By referring to this poem and to at least one other poem by Carol Ann Duffy, show how she explores the theme of love.

8

OR

Text 2 – Poetry

If you choose this text you may not attempt a question on Poetry in Section 2.
Read the extract below and then attempt the following questions.

Hyena by Edwin Morgan

The extract is from Hyena *(the first 25 lines).*

I am waiting for you.
I have been travelling all morning through the bush
and not eaten.
I am lying at the edge of the bush
5   on a dusty path that leads from the burnt-out kraal.
I am panting, it is midday, I found no water-hole.
I am very fierce without food and although my eyes
are screwed to slits against the sun
you must believe I am prepared to spring.

10   What do you think of me?
I have a rough coat like Africa.
I am crafty with dark spots
like the bush-tufted plains of Africa.
I sprawl as a shaggy bundle of gathered energy
15   like Africa sprawling in its waters.
I trot, I lope, I slaver, I am a ranger.
I hunch my shoulders. I eat the dead.

Do you like my song?
When the moon pours hard and cold on the veldt
20   I sing, and I am the slave of darkness.
Over the stone walls and the mud walls and the ruined places
and the owls, the moonlight falls.
I sniff a broken drum. I bristle. My pelt is silver.
I howl my song to the moon – up it goes.

25   Would you meet me there in the waste places?

Questions

MARKS

39 By referring to **two** poetic techniques in lines 1–9, show how the poet makes the hyena sound threatening.

4

40 Explain how the sentence structure in lines 10–17 enhances the poet's description of the hyena. Refer to **two** examples in your answer.

4

41 By referring to lines 18–25, explain how the poet's use of language conveys the harshness of the hyena's world. Refer to **two** examples in your answer.

4

42 With close textual reference, show how *Hyena* **is similar or is not similar** to at least one other poem or poems by Morgan. You may refer to language and/or ideas in your answer.

8

OR

Text 3 – Poetry

If you choose this text you may not attempt a question on Poetry in Section 2. Read the poem below and then attempt the following questions.

Basking Shark by Norman MacCaig

To stub an oar on a rock where none should be,
To have it rise with a slounge out of the sea
Is a thing that happened once (too often) to me.

But not too often – though enough. I count as gain
5   That I once met, on a sea tin-tacked with rain,
That roomsized monster with a matchbox brain.

He displaced more than water. He shoggled me
Centuries back – this decadent townee
Shook on a wrong branch of his family tree.

10   Swish up the dirt and, when it settles, a spring
Is all the clearer. I saw me, in one fling,
Emerging from the slime of everything.

So who's the monster? The thought made me grow pale
For twenty seconds while, sail after sail,
15   The tall fin slid away and then the tail.

Questions

43 By referring to the whole poem, explain in your own words what the poet's encounter with the shark made him reflect on.

2

44 By referring to lines 1–3, explain one way the poet suggests the encounter was quite alarming.

2

45 Show how any **one** poetic technique in line 6 adds impact to the description of the shark.

2

46 Choose any **two** examples of the poet's use of language in lines 7–9 which you find effective. Justify your choices in detail.

4

47 What impression does the last stanza (lines 13–15) create of the poet's feelings about the shark? Support your opinion with reference to the text.

2

48 With close textual reference, show how this poem **is similar or is not similar** to another poem or poems by MacCaig you have studied. You may refer to language and/or ideas in your answer.

8

OR

Text 4 – Poetry

If you choose this text you may not attempt a question on Poetry in Section 2.

Read the poem below and then attempt the following questions.

Lucozade by Jackie Kay

My mum is on a high bed next to sad chrysanthemums.
'Don't bring flowers, they only wilt and die.'
I am scared my mum is going to die
on the bed next to the sad chrysanthemums.

5   She nods off and her eyes go back in her head.
Next to her bed is a bottle of Lucozade.
'Orange nostalgia, that's what that is,' she says.
'Don't bring Lucozade either,' then fades.

'The whole day was a blur, a swarm of eyes.
10   Those doctors with their white lies.
Did you think you could cheer me up with a *Woman's Own*?
Don't bring magazines, too much about size.'

My mum wakes up, groggy and low.

'What I want to know,' she says, 'is this:

15 where's the big brandy, the generous gin, the Bloody Mary,

the biscuit tin, the chocolate gingers, the dirty big meringue?'

I am sixteen; I've never tasted a Bloody Mary.

'Tell your father to bring a luxury,' says she.

'Grapes have no imagination, they're just green.

20 Tell him: stop the neighbours coming.'

I clear her cupboard in Ward 10B, Stobhill Hospital.

I leave, bags full, Lucozade, grapes, oranges,

sad chrysanthemums under my arms,

weighted down. I turn round, wave with her flowers.

25 My mother, on her high hospital bed, waves back.

Her face is light and radiant, dandelion hours.

Her sheets billow and whirl. She is beautiful.

Next to her the empty table is divine.

I carry the orange nostalgia home singing an old song.

Questions

MARKS

49 Look at lines 1–12. Explain **two** ways the poet makes clear the mother's
negative mood.

4

50 Show how the poet's use of language in lines 13–20 makes a clear contrast
between 'grapes' and the 'luxury' the mother asks for.

4

51 By referring to **two** examples of the language used in lines 21–29, show how
the poem ends on a positive note.

4

52 By referring to this poem and to at least one other poem by Jackie Kay, show
how she explores the theme of relationships across generations.

8

[End of section 1]

Section 2 – Critical Essay – 20 marks

Attempt **ONE** question from the following genres – Drama, Prose, Poetry, Film and Television Drama, or Language.

Your answer must be on a different genre from that chosen in Section 1.

You should spend approximately 45 minutes on this Section.

Drama

Answers to questions on Drama should refer to the text and to such relevant features as characterisation, key scene(s), structure, climax, theme, plot, conflict, setting ...

1   Choose a play in which there is conflict between characters or between groups of characters or within one character.
    Describe the conflict and then, by referring to appropriate techniques, go on to explain why the conflict is important to the development of the play as a whole.

2   Choose a play in which there is one scene you consider to be a turning point.
    Describe briefly what happens at this turning point and then, by referring to appropriate techniques, go on to explain how it makes an impact on the play as a whole.

Prose

Answers to questions on Prose should refer to the text and to such relevant features as characterisation, setting, language, key incident(s), climax, turning point, plot, structure, narrative technique, theme, ideas, description ...

3   Choose a novel **or** short story which ends in a way you think is effective.
    Give a brief account of what happens at the end and then, by referring to appropriate techniques, explain why you think the ending is effective.

4   Choose a novel **or** a short story **or** a work of non-fiction which deals with an important human issue (such as prejudice, the conflict between good and evil, loss of freedom, hatred between individuals or groups, abuse of power).
    By referring to appropriate techniques, show how the writer explores this issue.

Poetry

Answers to questions on Poetry should refer to the text and to such relevant features as word choice, tone, imagery, structure, content, rhythm, rhyme, theme, sound, ideas ...

5   Choose a poem in which the poet creates a particular mood or atmosphere.
    By referring to poetic techniques, show how the poet creates this mood or atmosphere.

6   Choose a poem which describes an incident or an event or an encounter.
    By referring to poetic techniques, show how the poet creates the description.

Film and Television Drama

Answers to questions on Film and Television Drama should refer to the text and to such relevant features as use of camera, key sequence, characterisation, mise-en-scène, editing, setting, music/ sound, special effects, plot, dialogue ...

7   Choose the opening **or** closing scene or sequence from a film **or** television drama.*
By referring to appropriate techniques, explain why you find it an effective way to start or to finish the film or television drama.*

8   Choose a film **or** television drama* in which a character has to overcome a number of difficulties.
By referring to appropriate techniques, explain how successful the character is in overcoming these difficulties.

   * 'television drama' includes a single play, a series or a serial.

Language

Answers to questions on Language should refer to the text and to such relevant features as register, accent, dialect, slang, jargon, vocabulary, tone, abbreviation ...

9   Consider the specialised language of any specific group of people.
By referring to specific examples and to appropriate techniques, explain in what ways the language is distinctive and what benefit(s) the group gains from the use of this language.

10   Choose a print or non-print text which sets out to persuade people.
By referring to specific examples and to appropriate techniques, explain how the text engages the reader or viewer.

[End of section 2]

[End of question paper]

National 5
English

Paper 1: Reading for Understanding, Analysis and Evaluation

Duration: 1 hour

Total marks: 30

Attempt ALL questions.

Write your answers clearly in the answer booklet provided. In the answer booklet you must clearly identify the question number you are attempting.

Use **blue** or **black** ink.

Before leaving the examination room you must give your answer booklet to the Invigilator; if you do not you may lose all the marks for this paper.

Why didn't people smile in old photos?

From the time that photography was invented in 1839, portraiture (the likeness of a person, especially the face) was at the heart of its appeal. A noticeable feature of these early photographic portraits is that smiles are grimly absent from them. If you look, for example, at a famous old photograph of a young girl taken in 1852, you see her posed for the camera,
5   her head slightly turned, giving the lens a steady, confident, unsmiling look. She is preserved forever as a very serious girl indeed.

That severity is everywhere in Victorian photographs. Charles Darwin, by all accounts a warm character and a loving, playful parent, looks frozen in glumness in photographs. In Julia Margaret Cameron's great 1867 portrait of the astronomer John Frederick William Herschel,
10   his deep melancholy introspection and wild hair kissed by the light give him the air of a Shakespearean tragic hero.

Why did our ancestors, from unknown sitters for family portraits to the great and famous, become so mirthless in front of the lens? The apparently obvious answer is that they are freezing their faces in order to keep still for the long exposure times, but you don't have
15   to look very long at these unsmiling old photos to see how incomplete that answer is. In Julia Margaret Cameron's portrait of the poet Tennyson, he broods and dreams, his face a shadowed mask of genius. This is not simply a technical quirk. It's an aesthetic and emotional choice.

People in the past were not necessarily more gloomy than we are. They did not go around
20   in a perpetual state of sorrow – though they might be forgiven for doing so, in a world with much higher mortality rates than in the west today, and medicine that was puny indeed by our standards. In fact, the Victorians had a sense of humour even about the darkest aspects of their society. Jerome K Jerome's book *Three Men in a Boat* is a fascinating insight into the Victorian sense of humour – it's rollicking and irreverent. When the narrator drinks some
25   water from the river Thames, his friends chaff him that he will probably catch cholera. It's a

startling joke to make in 1889 just a few decades after cholera had ravaged London. Chaucer wrote *The Canterbury Tales*, which can still raise laughs today, in the fourteenth century, the century of the Black Death and the Hundred Years War. Jane Austen found plenty to giggle about in the era of the Napoleonic wars.

30 Laughter and jollity were not just common in the past but institutionalised far more than they are today, from medieval carnivals in which entire communities indulged in riotous comic antics to Georgian printshops where people gathered to look at the latest funnies. Far from suppressing festivals and fun, the Victorians, who invented photography, also created Christmas as the secular feast it is today.

35 So the severity of people in 19th-century photographs cannot be evidence of generalised gloom and depression. This was not a society in permanent despair. Instead, the true answer has to do with attitudes to portraiture itself.

People who posed for early photographs, from earnest middle-class families recording their status to celebrities captured by the lens, understood it as a significant moment. Photography
40 was still rare. Having your picture taken was not something that happened every day. For many people it might be a once-in-a-lifetime experience.

Posing for the camera, in other words, did not seem that different from having your portrait painted. It was cheaper, quicker (even with those slow exposure times) and meant that people who never had a chance to be painted could now be portrayed; but people seem to have
45 taken it seriously in the same way they would a painted portrait. This was not a 'snap'. Like a portrait painting, it was intended as a timeless record of a person.

Oil portraits of long ago are not that packed with smiles, either. Rembrandt's portraits would look very different if everyone was smiling in them. In fact they are full of the consciousness of mortality and the mystery of existence – nothing to smile about there. Look at the
50 intimately serious portraits painted by Velazquez or Titian or indeed most of the painted portraits in any museum and there aren't many smiley faces.

For the most part, melancholy and introspection haunt the oil portrait and this sense of the seriousness of life passes on from painting into early photography, which, I think, makes the old photographs so much more moving than modern ones. For what still survives in Victorian
55 photography is the grandeur and gravitas of traditional portraiture.

Today, we take so many smiling snaps that the idea of anyone finding true depth and poetry in most of them is absurd. Photos are about being social. We want to communicate ourselves as happy social people. So we smile, laugh and cavort in endless and endlessly shared selfies. A grinning selfie is the opposite of a serious portrait. It's just a momentary performance of
60 happiness. It has zero profundity and therefore zero artistic value. As a human document it is disturbingly throwaway. (In fact, not even solid enough to throw away – just press delete).

How beautiful and haunting old photographs are in comparison with our silly selfies. Those unsmiling people probably had as much fun as we do, if not more. But they felt no hysterical need to prove it with pictures. Instead, when they posed for a photograph, they thought about
65 time, death and memory. The presence of those grave realities in old photographs makes them worth far more than our inanely happy Instagram snaps.

Jonathan Jones, in the Guardian

Questions

MARKS

1 Look at lines 1–11, and then explain **in your own words two** key points the writer is making about early photographic portraits.

2

2 Referring to **two** examples of the writer's **word choice** in lines 7–11, explain how the appearance of early photographs is made clear.

4

3 Look at lines 12–18, and then explain **in your own words** the **two** answers the writer gives to the question he asks in lines 12–13.

2

4 Look at lines 19–34, and then summarise, **using your own words** as far as possible, the evidence the writer gives that 'People in the past were not necessarily more gloomy than we are'.

You should make **five** key points in your answer.

5

5 Explain why the paragraph in lines 35–37 provides an appropriate link at this point in the passage.

2

6 Look at lines 38–51, and then explain **in your own words two** similarities between early photographs and having a portrait painted, and **two** differences between them.

4

7 Look at lines 52–55, and then explain how **two** examples of the writer's **word choice** demonstrate his liking for old photographs.

4

8 Look at lines 56–61, and then explain how **two** examples of the language used demonstrate his dislike of modern photography.

4

9 Explain why the last paragraph (lines 62–66) provides an effective conclusion to the passage as a whole.

3

[End of question paper]

Paper 2: Critical Reading

Duration: 90 minutes

Total marks: 40

SECTION 1 – Scottish Text – 20 marks

Read an extract from a Scottish text you have previously studied.

Choose ONE text from either

Part A – Drama   Pages 59—64

or

Part B – Prose   Pages 65—71

or

Part C – Poetry   Pages 72—77

Attempt ALL the questions for your chosen text.

SECTION 2 – Critical Essay – 20 marks

Attempt ONE question from the following genres – Drama, Prose, Poetry, Film and Television Drama, or Language.

Your answer must be on a different genre from that chosen in Section 1.

You should spend approximately 45 minutes on each Section.

Write your answers clearly in the answer booklet provided. In the answer booklet you must clearly identify the question number you are attempting.

Use **blue** or **black** ink.

Before leaving the examination room you must give your answer booklet to the Invigilator; if you do not you may lose all the marks for this paper.

Section 1 – Scottish Text – 20 marks

Part A – Scottish Text – Drama

Text 1 – Drama

If you choose this text you may not attempt a question on Drama in Section 2.

Read the extract below and then attempt the following questions.

Bold Girls by Rona Munro

The extract is from Scene Two, in the club. Cassie is dancing alone, and Nora persuades Marie to join her.

Marie crosses over and joins Cassie who beams, applauding her. Marie starts shuffling cautiously from foot to foot

	CASSIE:	I'm telling you this is a great diet Marie, you really feel the benefit of the gin.
	MARIE:	Well maybe you should go easy now, Cassie.
5	CASSIE:	Oh I'm a long way from lockjawed.

Nora is beckoning at them frantically

	MARIE:	Your mummy's asking us to come and sit down.
	CASSIE:	The song's just started.

Marie glances round nervously

10		What? Are they all watching us?
	MARIE:	They are.
	CASSIE:	Let them.
	MARIE:	(*with a shaky laugh*) Feel a bit like the last meat pie in the shop out here, Cassie.
15	CASSIE:	Well let them stay hungry. They can just look and think what they like.
	MARIE:	Cassie, what's wrong?
	CASSIE:	Oh, I'm just bad Marie, didn't you know?
	MARIE:	No. I never knew that.
	CASSIE:	You remember that wee girl in Turf Lodge, the one Martin couldn't get enough
20		of? She was a decent wee girl. She's bad now. Ask my mummy.
	MARIE:	Have you had words?
	CASSIE:	He's out in less than a year, Marie.
	MARIE:	*Martin*!?
	CASSIE:	Joe.
25	MARIE:	I know. It'll be all right Cassie.

They stop dancing, they look at each other

		It'll be all right, Cassie.

	CASSIE:	I tell you Marie I can't stand the *smell* of him. The greasy, grinning, beer bellied smell of him. And he's winking away about all he's been dreaming
30		of, wriggling his fat fingers over me like I'm a poke of chips – I don't want him in the house in my *bed*, Marie.
	MARIE:	You'll cope.
	CASSIE:	Oh I'm just bad. I am.
	MARIE:	Don't. Don't say that about yourself.
35	CASSIE:	I'll go crazy.
	MARIE:	I won't let you. You won't get a chance Cassie, I'll just be across the road, I won't let you go crazy. You just see what you'll get if you try it.

Slowly Cassie smiles at her

(*Putting a hand on Cassie's arm*) Now will you come and sit down?

Questions

MARKS

1 By referring closely to lines 1–15, show how the playwright contrasts the characters of Marie and Cassie through their language **and** their actions.

4

2 Explain how the dialogue in lines 16–39 reveals aspects of the relationship between Marie and Cassie. You should refer to **two** examples.

4

3 By referring to **two** examples of the language in lines 28–31, show how Cassie reveals her attitude to Joe.

4

4 The relationship between Marie and Cassie is central to *Bold Girls*. With reference to the extract and elsewhere in the play, show how the playwright presents this relationship.

8

OR

Text 2 – Drama

If you choose this text you may not attempt a question on Drama in Section 2.

Read the extract below and then attempt the following questions.

Sailmaker by Alan Spence

The extract is from the closing moments of Act One.

(DAVIE *and* BILLY *enter, opposite sides of stage*)

	BILLY:	What's up wi your face?
		(DAVIE *shakes head*)
		What's the matter?
5	DAVIE:	Ah just got ma jotters. Week's notice.
	BILLY:	Jesus Christ! What for?

	DAVIE:	Ach! They're saying the book's a dead loss. They're gonnae shut it awthegether. Put the sheriff's officers on tae the folk that still owe money.
	BILLY:	Bastards.
10	DAVIE:	Getting that doin just finished it. Losin the money an the ledgers an everythin.
	BILLY:	But that wasnae your fault!
	DAVIE:	Try tellin *them* that! So that's me. Scrubbed. Again. Laid off. Redundant. Services no longer required. Just like that. Ah don't know. Work aw yer
15		days an what've ye got tae show for it? Turn roon an kick ye in the teeth. Ah mean, what *have* ye got when ye come right down tae it. Nothin.
	BILLY:	Ah might be able to get ye a start in our place. Cannae promise mind ye. An if there was anything it wouldnae be much. Maybe doin yer sweeper up or that.
20	DAVIE:	Anythin's better than nothin.
	BILLY:	An once yer in the place, ye never know. Somethin better might come up.
	DAVIE:	(*Dead*) Aye.
	BILLY:	Likes ae a storeman's job or that.
	DAVIE:	Aye.
25	BILLY:	We never died a winter yet, eh?

(DAVIE *nods*. BILLY *exits*)

| | DAVIE: | Scrubbed. Get yer jacket on. Pick up yer cards. On yer way pal! Out the door. |

(ALEC *is playing with yacht, positions fid like bowsprit, bow like mast, tries to make 'sail' with*
30 *cellophane, can't hold all the separate bits, drops them.* DAVIE *comes in behind him*)

	DAVIE:	Bit of bad news son.
	(*Pause*)	
		Ah've lost ma job. They gave me ma books.
	ALEC:	What'll we dae?
35	DAVIE:	Billy says he might be able to fix me up wi something. Wouldnae be much. (*Shrugs*) Better than nothin. Ach, that was a lousy job anyway. Ah'm better off out ae it. Whatever happens.
		Place is a right mess eh. Amazin how it gets on top of ye.
	ALEC:	Ah'll shove this in the Glory Hole. Out the road.
40	(*Folds up cellophane, puts tools in bag and picks up bow, yacht, carries the lot and exits*)
	DAVIE:	Ach aye. No to worry. Never died a winter yet.

Questions

5 Summarise what is said between Davie and Billy in lines 2–25. Make at least **four** key points.

4

6 Explain how the sentence structure of lines 13–16 helps the audience to understand how Davie is feeling.

2

7 Explain how the dialogue in lines 17–25 emphasises the difference between Davie and Billy.

2

8 Explain what is revealed about **two** aspects of Davie's personality in lines 32–38.

4

9 By referring to the extract and to elsewhere in the play, show how the playwright presents the character of Davie.

8

OR

Text 3 – Drama

If you choose this text you may not attempt a question on Drama in Section 2.

Read the extract below and then attempt the following questions.

Tally's Blood by Ann Marie Di Mambro

The extract is from Act One, Scene Two. It is 1939. Lucia is five years old.

	MASSIMO:	Listen, Rosie, I thought you went to Glasgow to buy yourself a new coat.
	ROSINELLA:	Oh, but see when I saw that wee dress I just had to get her it. My heart's breaking for that wee lassie these days.
	MASSIMO:	She's just a wean. She'll no understand.
5	ROSINELLA:	But she's lovely in it, isn't she?
	MASSIMO:	Don't get me wrong. I don't grudge the wean a frock. God forbid. It's just you I'm worried about. Last year when I gave you money for a coat you bought jumpers to send to Italy.
	ROSINELLA:	So?

10 *Massimo smiles with great affection, squeezes her cheek between his thumb and forefinger.*

| | MASSIMO: | So what have I to do with you, you daft wee besom, you? |

Lucia comes back carrying her schoolbag: Massimo takes it from her.

| | MASSIMO: | Oh, is this what I got? Let me see. Oh, that's great, so it is. Just what I was needing for bringing home the tatties. Oh here, it's awfy wee. You better |
| 15 | | just take it, Lucia. |

He pretends to put it on: Lucia giggles.

| | LUCIA: | Uncle Massimo, you're awful silly. |
| | ROSINELLA: | Now away you go, Lucia, and take off your lovely dress. |

	LUCIA:	(*Mood changing/petulant*) I want to keep it on.
20	ROSINELLA:	(*Coaxing*) You need to take it off, love.
	LUCIA:	No.
	MASSIMO:	Keep it nice for something special.
	LUCIA:	No.
	ROSINELLA:	If you take it off now I'll let you wear it to mass this Sunday.
25	LUCIA:	I want to keep it on.
	ROSINELLA:	Come on, hen.
	LUCIA:	I'm keeping it on, I says.
	MASSIMO:	You better no let her away with that.
	ROSINELLA:	Come on, darling, we'll get you changed.
30	LUCIA:	(*Starting to shout*) No, no, no.
	ROSINELLA:	(*Voice raised but pleading*) Now Lucia!

Massimo glances over shoulder in direction of front shop.

	LUCIA:	I don't want to. I don't want to.
	MASSIMO:	Sshh! You two. I've got customers out there. (*To Lucia*) Do what your Auntie
35		Rosinella tells you, darling, there's a good girl.

Rosinella takes Lucia's arm to lead her away.

	ROSINELLA:	Come on, Lucia.

Lucia starts to scream and pull back.

	LUCIA:	No, no, no, leave me alone, I want to keep it on. I want to keep it on. No –
40		no – no –

Rosinella and Massimo look helplessly at each other. Massimo also keeps glancing in direction of shop, anxious to get back.

	ROSINELLA:	(*Appealing*) Massimo.
	MASSIMO:	Maybe you're being too hard on her.
45	ROSINELLA:	Me?
	MASSIMO:	Why no let her keep it on for a wee while, eh?
	ROSINELLA:	Just a wee while, then, OK.

Lucia controls her sobs (she's won).

	LUCIA:	OK.

C

Questions

10 Summarise what happens in this extract. Make at least **three** key points.

3

11 Identify **two** aspects of Rosinella's character that the audience learns from lines 1–9.

2

12 By referring to **two** examples from lines 18–49, explain how the playwright makes Lucia's behaviour typical of a young child.

4

13 At this stage in the play the characters have only been in Scotland for three years, but their speech shows clear signs of Scottish words and phrases. Quote **three** examples of this from anywhere in the extract.

3

14 The extract looks at the relationship between Lucia and her aunt and uncle. With reference to this extract and to elsewhere in the play, show how their relationship is portrayed.

8

Section 1 – Scottish Text – 20 marks

Part B – Scottish Text – Prose

Text 1 – Prose

If you choose this text you may not attempt a question on Prose in Section 2.

Read the extract below and then attempt the following questions.

The Cone-Gatherers by Robin Jenkins

The extract is from Chapter 5. Calum and Neil are high in a tree; they hear Duror starting to climb towards them.

They heard the scrapes and thumps of his nailed boots on the rungs and then on the branches. A branch cracked suddenly. He exclaimed as if in anger, and paused for a full minute. When he resumed he climbed even more slowly than before. Soon he stopped again. He was still a long way below.

5   They waited, but he did not start to climb again. For three or four minutes they waited. Still he remained motionless and silent. One of the dogs barked unhappily.

They thought he must have climbed as high as he wished, and now was admiring the view of the loch. After all, the tree was not private just because they happened to be in it; the ladder, too, belonged to the estate. At the same time Neil felt curiously embarrassed and could not

10   think to start gathering cones again. Calum kept shivering.

They were far from guessing the truth, that Duror had ceased to climb because of fear; that, weak and dizzy and full of shame, he was clinging with ignominious tightness; that the dread of the descent was making him sick; and that he had almost forgotten his purpose in ascending to them.

15   At last Neil had to end the suspense.

'Hello, Mr. Duror,' he called. 'It's a grand day, isn't it?'

No reply came.

Neil tried again.

'Do you want to talk to us about something?' he shouted.

20   This time, after another long delay, there was a reply. They were surprised by the mildness of his voice. It was so faint too they had to strain to hear it.

'I've got a message for you,' he said.

'A message? Is it from Mr. Tulloch?'

There was a pause. 'Aye, from him.'

25   'Have we to go back home, to Ardmore?' cried Neil hopefully.

'You know these woods belong to Lady Runcie-Campbell?'

'We know that.'

'She wants you as beaters in a deer drive this afternoon.'

Neil was shocked.

30 'But we're here to gather cones,' he yelled. 'She can't order us about. She's not our mistress.'

'She telephoned Tulloch. He said you've to work for her this afternoon.'

'How could he? Didn't he tell us we'd to gather every cone we could? Didn't he ask us to work as much overtime as we liked? What's the good of all that if we're to be taken away for deer
35 drives.' Neil's voice grew hoarse with indignation. 'My brother's never asked to take part in deer hunts,' he shouted. 'Mr. Tulloch knows that. I don't believe he knows anything about this. It's just a trick to get us to work for the lady.'

Duror was silent. His triumph was become a handful of withered leaves. When he had seen the ladder, he had thought how gratifying it would be to deliver the deadly message to them
40 in the eyrie where they fancied themselves safe. He had not anticipated this lightheadedness, this heaving of the stationary tree, this treachery of nature, this sickening of his very will to hate. He had never dreamed that he would not be able to do once only what the hunchback did several times a day. It seemed to him that he must therefore be far more ill and decayed than he had thought. He was like a tree still straight, still showing green leaves; but
45 underground death was creeping along the roots.

Questions

MARKS

15 Using your own words as far as possible, summarise what happens in this extract from the novel. Make at least **four** key points.

4

16 By referring to **one** example, show how the writer creates a tense mood in the first two paragraphs (lines 1–6).

2

17 Look carefully at what Neil says in lines 16–37. Referring closely to the text, show how his attitude towards Duror goes through at least **two** changes.

4

18 Explain what the image in the last sentence of the extract tells you about Duror.

2

19 By referring to the extract and to elsewhere in the novel, show how the conflict between Duror and the cone-gatherers is explored.

8

OR

Text 2 – Prose

If you choose this text you may not attempt a question on Prose in Section 2.

Read the extract below and then attempt the following questions.

The Testament of Gideon Mack by James Robertson

The extract is from Chapter 25. Gideon is visiting Catherine Craigie for the first time. He has rung the bell twice, but nothing has happened ...

'Just come in, for heaven's sake. It's not locked.'

I leaned forward to open the door and noticed a handwritten card taped to the wall of the vestibule: *Please ring and enter. If locked go away.*

'Can't you read?' the voice said as I let myself in.

5   'Sorry,' I said, 'I only just saw it. I'm sorry if I've interrupted you.'

'You shouldn't have rung the bell if you didn't want to interrupt me,' Miss Craigie said. 'I don't sit around waiting for visitors all day, you know. Oh, it's you.'

She said these last words not apologetically but with added distaste. It was dark in the hallway, and I could not make out the expression on her face, but the tone of voice told me all
10   I needed to know. I'd been well warned by various members of my flock: Catherine Craigie thought that the Kirk, by and large, had been, was and always would be a scabrous outbreak on the flesh of Scotland.

I was wearing my dog collar – I was planning to make some other calls that evening – and assumed that this was the cause of her aggravation. I tapped it with my forefinger.

15   'It doesn't make you a bad person,' I said.

'Hmph,' she retorted. 'It doesn't make you a good one either. What do you want?'

'I've come to say hello, Miss Craigie. I've been here nearly four years and I feel we should have met by now.' This didn't seem to impress her. 'And I want to ask you some questions about the standing stones. I've been reading your book.'

20   'Well, it's all in there, so I don't see why you need to come bothering me if you haven't taken the trouble to read it properly.'

'Supplementary questions,' I said. 'Arising out of what I've read.'

'I know what a supplementary question is,' she said. 'Such as?'

I'd had the forethought to compose something beforehand.

25   'Well, it seems to me, in all this debate about pre-Christian and Christianised Picts, that we forget that they were under pressure from two rival Christianities, the Celtic and the Roman – the Scots in the west and the Northumbrians in the south. And I wondered what bearing that might have had on the symbols on the stones.'

During this speech her head inclined towards me like a bird's listening for danger, or for a
30   worm. Later, I realised that this stance was in part due to her illness, which prevented her from moving her neck very much. She was standing halfway down the hallway, holding on to a tall wooden plant-stand positioned in the middle of a large rug. There was no plant on the plant-stand and it took me a moment to understand the reason for its location: the lay-out of the hall, from the front door to the foot of the stairs and on towards the back lobby, was a
35   kind of domestic rock-face, with hand-holds and rest points along the way, some pre-existing and some strategically placed: the plant-stand, a chair, a table, a stool, a shelf, the banister end, radiators. This horizontal climbing-wall was how Miss Craigie managed to get around her house.

Questions

20 By referring to **two** examples from lines 1–12, show how the writer portrays Miss Craigie as an intimidating character.

4

21 Show how the dialogue in lines 13–23 conveys the friction between Gideon and Miss Craigie. You should refer to **two** examples.

4

22 Show how the writer's sentence structure and imagery in lines 29–38 help to describe the layout of Miss Craigie's hallway.

4

23 By referring to the extract and to elsewhere in the novel, show how the character of Miss Craigie is important in *The Testament of Gideon Mack*.

8

OR

Text 3 – Prose

If you choose this text you may not attempt a question on Prose in Section 2.

Read the extract below and then attempt the following questions.

Kidnapped by Robert Louis Stevenson

The extract is from Chapter 10 – The Siege of the Roundhouse. *David and Alan fight off the first assault.*

I do not know if I was what you call afraid; but my heart beat like a bird's, both quick and little; and there was a dimness came before my eyes which I continually rubbed away, and which continually returned. As for hope, I had none; but only a darkness of despair and a sort of anger against all the world that made me long to sell my life as dear as

5   I was able. I tried to pray, I remember, but that same hurry of my mind, like a man running, would not suffer me to think upon the words; and my chief wish was to have the thing begin and be done with it.

It came all of a sudden when it did, with a rush of feet and a roar, and then a shout from Alan, and a sound of blows and some one crying out as if hurt. I looked back over my

10   shoulder, and saw Mr Shuan in the doorway, crossing blades with Alan.

'That's him that killed the boy!' I cried.

'Look to your window!' said Alan; and as I turned back to my place, I saw him pass his sword through the mate's body.

It was none too soon for me to look to my own part; for my head was scarce back at the

15   window, before five men carrying a spare yard for a battering-ram, ran past me and took post to drive the door in. I had never fired with a pistol in my life, and not often with a gun; far less against a fellow-creature. But it was now or never; and just as they swang the yard, I cried out, 'Take that!' and shot into their midst.

I must have hit one of them, for he sang out and gave back a step, and the rest stopped

20   as if a little disconcerted. Before they had time to recover, I sent another ball over their heads; and at my third shot (which went as wide as the second) the whole party threw down the yard and ran for it.

Then I looked round again into the deck-house. The whole place was full of the smoke of my own firing, just as my ears seemed to be burst with the noise of the shots. But there was

25 Alan, standing as before; only now his sword was running blood to the hilt, and himself so swelled with triumph and fallen into so fine an attitude, that he looked to be invincible. Right before him on the floor was Mr Shuan, on his hands and knees; the blood was pouring from his mouth, and he was sinking slowly lower, with a terrible, white face; and just as I looked, some of those from behind caught hold of him by the heels and dragged him bodily out of the

30 round-house. I believe he died as they were doing it.

'There's one of your Whigs for ye!' cried Alan; and then turning to me, he asked if I had done much execution.

I told him I had winged one, and thought it was the captain.

'And I've settled two,' says he. 'No, there's not enough blood let; they'll be back again. To your

35 watch, David. This was but a dram before meat.'

Questions

MARKS

24 Identify briefly **two** different emotions David feels in lines 1–7.

2

25 By referring to the language used in lines 8–22, explain **two** ways by which the writer makes the events dramatic and exciting.

4

26 By referring to lines 23–32, explain **two** impressions you are given of Alan Breck's personality.

4

27 'This was but a dram before meat.' (line 35). Explain in your own words what Alan means by this.

2

28 By referring to the extract and to elsewhere in the novel, show how the relationship between David and Alan Breck develops.

8

OR

Text 4 – Prose

If you choose this text you may not attempt a question on Prose in Section 2.

Read the extract below and then attempt the following questions.

In Church by Iain Crichton Smith

The extract is from near the end of In Church.

'At the age of eighteen I was forced into the army to fight for what they call one's country. I did not know what this was since my gaze was always directed inward and not outward. I was put among men whom I despised and feared – they fornicated and drank and spat and lived filthily. Yet they were my comrades in arms.

5 'I was being shot at by strangers. I was up to my knees in green slime. I was harassed by rats. I entered trenches to find the dead buried in the walls. Once, however, on a clear starry

night at Christmas time we had a truce. This lasted into the following day. We – Germans and English – showed each other our photographs, though I had none. We, that is, the others, played football. At the end of it a German officer came up to us and said: "You had better get
10   back to your dugouts: we are starting a barrage at 13.00 hours." He consulted his watch and we went back to our trenches after we had shaken hands with each other.

'One day I could bear no more of the killing and I ran away. And I came here, Lord. And now I should like to say something to you, Lord. I was never foolish enough to think that I understood your ways. Nevertheless I thought you were on the side of the good and the
15   innocent. Now I no longer believe so. You may strike me dead with your lightning – I invite you to do so – but I think that will not happen. All these years, Lord, you have cheated me. You in your immense absence.' He paused a moment as if savouring the phrase. 'Your immense absence. As for me, I have been silent for a year without love, without hope. I have lived like an animal, I who was willing to give my all to you. Lord, do you know what it is to be alone?
20   For in order to live we need language and human beings.

'I think, Lord, that I hate you. I hate you for inventing the world and then abandoning it. I hate you because you have not intervened to save the world.

'I hate you because you are as indifferent as the generals. I hate you because of my weakness.

'I hate you, God, because of what you have done to mankind.'

Questions

29   Explain how the language used in lines 1–4 makes clear how much the speaker dislikes army life. Refer to **two** examples in your answer.

4

30   Explain **two** ways in which the writer uses contrast in lines 5–11 to emphasise the strangeness of the Christmas truce.

4

31   By referring to lines 12–24, explain in your own words as far as possible why the speaker is angry at God. You should make **four** key points.

4

32   By referring to the extract and to at least one other story by Crichton Smith, show how he creates tension between characters.

8

OR

Text 5 – Prose

If you choose this text you may not attempt a question on Prose in Section 2.

Read the extract below and then attempt the following questions.

Zimmerobics by Anne Donovan

The extract is from Zimmerobics.

And there's this constant feeling of awareness in every part of my body; jaggy pains in my elbows and knees, vertebrae grinding against one another, bits that used to fit together smoothly now clicking and crunking like the central-heating boiler starting up. I did once try to explain it to Catherine.

5 'It's like the shows, those games where you get a circle on a stick and you have to feed it along a piece of twisted wire, very carefully without touching it and, if you touch the wire a bell rings.'

'Uh-huh.' She is busy rearranging ornaments on the mantelpiece.

'It's like that. I have to do everything really slowly and carefully, otherwise it hurts.'

Catherine gave me one of her looks and said I should take more interest in things. She
10 knows I can't knit any more and reading tires me but she's always trying to get me to put photographs in albums or watch the TV.

'*Top Hat*'s on TV this afternoon,' she said as she was getting ready to leave. 'Fred Astaire and Ginger Rogers.'

'Oh, is it?'

15 'It starts at two-thirty and it's all set for you. I'm away for the two o'clock bus. See you on Friday.'

I didn't watch the film. I'd rather sit and daydream out of the window, lost inside my own head. Catherine can't understand as it's not in her nature to daydream or dawdle or drift. She's like an office stapler, precisely snapping shut, securing papers in the correct order forever. She never lets anything go. When she returned on Friday the first thing she said to me was:

20 'Did you enjoy the film?'

I was caught off my guard.

'The film?'

'*Top Hat* – you didn't watch it, did you? I knew you wouldn't. I don't know why I bother. You've no interest in anything outside yourself. You never even bother to go along to the dayroom.
25 There's three ladies sitting there now, having a wee chat. You could go and meet people.'

Catherine always pronounces 'meet' as if it were printed in capital letters. This was one of her favourite monologues, that I should MEET people in the dayroom. I knew I could shuffle along there with my Zimmer but I could never be bothered. There was bingo on Mondays and a drink on Saturday nights but I never went to either. She thinks I'm a snob, that I think I'm
30 better than these women but it's not that; it's just, I'd rather sit here.

Questions

MARKS

33 Look at lines 1–4. By referring to **two** examples of the writer's language, show how the narrator's physical discomfort is conveyed. 4

34 By referring to lines 5–15, explain **two** impressions you are given of Catherine's personality. 4

35 By referring to lines 16–30, show how the writer conveys the contrast between the narrator and her niece. 4

36 By referring to the extract and to at least one other story by Anne Donovan, show how the theme of conflict between characters is explored. 8

Section 1 – Scottish Text – 20 marks

Part C – Scottish Text – Poetry

Text 1 – Poetry

If you choose this text you may not attempt a question on Poetry in Section 2.
Read the extract below and then attempt the following questions.

Mrs Midas by Carol Ann Duffy
The extract is from Mrs Midas *(verses 5–8).*

It was then that I started to scream. He sank to his knees.
After we'd both calmed down, I finished the wine
on my own, hearing him out. I made him sit
on the other side of the room and keep his hands to himself.
5 I locked the cat in the cellar. I moved the phone.
The toilet I didn't mind. I couldn't believe my ears:

how he'd had a wish. Look, we all have wishes; granted.
But who has wishes granted? Him. Do you know about gold?
It feeds no one; aurum, soft, untarnishable; slakes
10 no thirst. He tried to light a cigarette; I gazed, entranced,
as the blue flame played on its luteous stem. At least,
I said, you'll be able to give up smoking for good.

Separate beds. In fact, I put a chair against my door,
near petrified. He was below, turning the spare room
15 into the tomb of Tutankhamun. You see, we were passionate then,
in those halcyon days; unwrapping each other, rapidly,
like presents, fast food. But now I feared his honeyed embrace,
the kiss that would turn my lips to a work of art.

And who, when it comes to the crunch, can live
20 with a heart of gold? That night, I dreamt I bore
his child, its perfect ore limbs, its little tongue
like a precious latch, its amber eyes
holding their pupils like flies. My dream-milk
burned in my breasts. I woke to the streaming sun.

Questions

MARKS

37 By referring to **two** examples in lines 1–12, show how the poet creates a light-hearted, humorous tone.

4

38 Show how the poet's use of language in lines 13–18 conveys the way the relationship between the speaker and her husband has changed. Refer to **two** examples in your answer.

4

39 By referring to **two** details in the speaker's dream (lines 20–24) explain how her fears are conveyed.

4

40 By referring to this poem and to at least one other poem by Carol Ann Duffy, show how she explores tension within a relationship **or** within an individual.

8

OR

Text 2 – Poetry

If you choose this text you may not attempt a question on Poetry in Section 2.
Read the poem below and then attempt the following questions.

Trio by Edwin Morgan

Coming up Buchanan Street, quickly, on a sharp winter evening

a young man and two girls, under the Christmas lights –

The young man carries a new guitar in his arms,

the girl on the inside carries a very young baby,

5 and the girl on the outside carries a chihuahua.

And the three of them are laughing, their breath rises

in a cloud of happiness, and as they pass

the boy says, 'Wait till he sees this but!'

The chihuahua has a tiny Royal Stewart tartan coat like a teapot-holder,

10 the baby in its white shawl is all bright eyes and mouth like favours in a fresh sweet cake,

the guitar swells out under its milky plastic cover, tied at the neck with silver tinsel tape and
           a brisk sprig of mistletoe.

Orphean sprig! Melting baby! Warm chihuahua!

The vale of tears is powerless before you.

15 Whether Christ is born, or is not born, you

put paid to fate, it abdicates

                          under the Christmas lights.

Monsters of the year

go blank, are scattered back,

20 can't bear this march of three.

– And the three have passed, vanished in the crowd

(yet not vanished, for in their arms they wind

the life of men and beasts, and music,

laughter ringing them round like a guard)

25 at the end of this winter's day.

Questions

41 By referring to **two** examples from lines 1–8, explain how the poet establishes a happy mood at the start of the poem.

4

42 Look at the descriptions in lines 9–12 of the chihuahua, the baby and the guitar. Choose any **two** of these and explain in detail how the poet's use of language creates an effective description.

4

43 In lines 13–25 the poet conveys his feelings about what he has just seen. In your own words, explain what these feelings are. You should make **four** key points.

4

44 By referring to this poem and to at least one other poem by Edwin Morgan, show how he transforms a simple event or situation into something special and thought-provoking.

8

OR

Text 3 – Poetry

If you choose this text you may not attempt a question on Poetry in Section 2. Read the poem below and then attempt the following questions.

Visiting Hour by Norman MacCaig

The hospital smell

combs my nostrils

as they go bobbing along

green and yellow corridors.

5 What seems a corpse

is trundled into a lift and vanishes

heavenward.

I will not feel, I will not
feel, until
10   I have to.

Nurses walk lightly, swiftly,
here and up and down and there,
their slender waists miraculously
carrying their burden
15   of so much pain, so
many deaths, their eyes
still clear after
so many farewells.

Ward 7. She lies
20   in a white cave of forgetfulness.
A withered hand
trembles on its stalk. Eyes move
behind eyelids too heavy
to raise. Into an arm wasted
25   of colour a glass fang is fixed,
not guzzling but giving.
And between her and me
distance shrinks till there is none left
but the distance of pain that neither she nor I
30   can cross.

She smiles a little at this
black figure in her white cave
who clumsily rises
in the round swimming waves of a bell
35   and dizzily goes off, growing fainter,
not smaller, leaving behind only
books that will not be read
and fruitless fruits.

Questions

45 Look at lines 1–10. By referring to **two** examples of the poet's use of language, explain how the speaker's discomfort is made clear.

4

46 Look at lines 11–18. By referring to **two** poetic techniques, show how the speaker's admiration for the nurses is conveyed.

4

47 Choose **one** example of imagery from lines 19–30 and explain how it adds to your understanding of the poem.

2

48 '... leaving behind only
books that will not be read
and fruitless fruits.' (lines 36–38)

Do you think this is a good way to end the poem? Justify your answer.

2

49 MacCaig's poems often describe deep personal feelings. By referring to this poem and to at least one other poem by MacCaig, show how he conveys these feelings.

8

OR

Text 4 – Poetry

If you choose this text you may not attempt a question on Poetry in Section 2.
Read the extract below and then attempt the following questions.

My Grandmother's Houses by Jackie Kay
The extract is Part 3 of My Grandmother's Houses.

By the time I am seven we are almost the same height.
She still walks faster, rushing me down the High Street
till we get to her cleaning house. The hall is huge.
Rooms lead off like an octopus's arms.
5 I sit in a room with a grand piano, top open –
a one-winged creature, whilst my gran polishes
for hours. Finally bored I start to pick some notes,
oh can you wash a sailor's shirt oh can you wash and clean
till my gran comes running, duster in hand.
10 I told you don't touch anything. The woman comes too;
the posh one all smiles that make goosepimples
run up my arms. Would you like to sing me a song?
Someone's crying my Lord Kumbaya. Lovely, she says,

beautiful child, skin the colour of café au lait.

15 'Café oh what? Hope she's not being any bother.'

Not at all. Not at all. You just get back to your work.

On the way back to her high rise I see her

like the hunchback of Notre Dame. Everytime I crouch

over a comic she slaps me. Sit up straight.

Questions

		MARKS
50	Identify **four** aspects of the grandmother's personality that emerge from the extract as a whole.	4
51	Choose **one** example of imagery from lines 4–7 and explain what it suggests about what is being described.	2
52	By referring closely to the language used in lines 10–16, explain how the poet conveys the personality of 'the woman'. Refer to **three** examples in your answer.	6
53	By referring to this poem and to at least one other poem by Jackie Kay, show how she creates vivid impressions of people.	8

[End of section 1]

Section 2 – Critical Essay – 20 marks

Attempt **ONE** question from the following genres – Drama, Prose, Poetry, Film and Television Drama, or Language.

Your answer must be on a different genre from that chosen in Section 1.

You should spend approximately 45 minutes on this Section.

Drama

Answers to questions on Drama should refer to the text and to such relevant features as characterisation, key scene(s), structure, climax, theme, plot, conflict, setting ...

1 Choose a play in which the playwright explores a theme which you feel is important.
By referring to appropriate techniques, show how effectively the playwright establishes and explores the theme.

2 Choose a play which you feel has an effective opening scene or an effective final scene.
Describe briefly what happens in the scene and then, by referring to appropriate techniques, explain why it is an effective way to start or to conclude the play as a whole.

Prose

Answers to questions on Prose should refer to the text and to such relevant features as characterisation, setting, language, key incident(s), climax, turning point, plot, structure, narrative technique, theme, ideas, description ...

3 Choose a novel **or** a short story in which a character is in conflict with another character or with a group of characters or with society as a whole.
By referring to appropriate techniques, show how the conflict arises and what effect it has on the character's fate in the novel or short story as a whole.

4 Choose a novel **or** short story **or** work of non-fiction which has a key incident or a turning point.
Give a brief account of the incident, and by referring to appropriate techniques, show how this incident is important to the text as a whole.

Poetry

Answers to questions on Poetry should refer to the text and to such relevant features as word choice, tone, imagery, structure, content, rhythm, rhyme, theme, sound, ideas ...

5 Choose a poem which made a deep impression on you.
By referring to poetic techniques, show how the poet made this deep impression.

6 Choose a poem which portrays an interesting character.
By referring to poetic techniques, show how the poet makes the character interesting.

Film and Television Drama

Answers to questions on Film and Television Drama should refer to the text and to such relevant features as use of camera, key sequence, characterisation, mise-en-scène, editing, setting, music/ sound, special effects, plot, dialogue ...

7 Choose a scene or sequence from a film **or** television drama* which you think is sad or exciting or moving or funny or frightening.
By referring to appropriate techniques, explain how the director leads you to feel this way.

8 Choose a film **or** television drama* which has a memorable main character.
By referring to appropriate techniques, explain how the character is presented in the film or television drama* as a whole.

   * 'television drama' includes a single play, a series or a serial.

Language

Answers to questions on Language should refer to the text and to such relevant features as register, accent, dialect, slang, jargon, vocabulary, tone, abbreviation ...

9 Choose **two** advertisements which aim to persuade you to change your opinion or to buy something or to change your behaviour.
By referring to specific examples, explain how successful the persuasive language is.

10 Consider the ways that young people use the internet to communicate and socialise, for example social networking sites or instant messaging or chat rooms or blogs.
By referring to specific examples and to appropriate techniques, explain how these communications differ from standard English and what their attractions are for young people.

[End of section 2]

[End of question paper]

National 5 English

Practice paper A

Paper 1: Reading for Understanding, Analysis and Evaluation

Sport is here to stay

Question	Expected response	Max. mark	Additional guidance
1	Candidates should explain fully why the first paragraph is an effective opening to the passage as a whole. Be aware of and award a mixed approach (i.e. ideas and language) to this question. Any three points for 3 marks.	3	■ it introduces the main topic of sport … (1) ■ … and how much of it there is (1) ■ it creates surprise/amusement at the sheer amount (1) Also accept: ■ use of first person (1) ■ use of list to demonstrate abundance of sport (1) ■ understatement of 'a fair bit' (1) ■ the density of proper names, numbers, abbreviations is almost confusing/disturbing (1)
2	Candidates should explain in their own words four ways in which the importance of sport has changed over the years. Any four points for 4 marks.	4	■ 30 years ago, no football on TV led to very little complaint (1) ■ today, it would cause uproar (1) ■ in mid-19th century, there were no major international/worldwide sporting events (1) ■ in mid-19th century, there were no organisations set up to control sport (1) ■ for a long time sport was not considered important (1) ■ for a long time sport was seen by churches as an unsuitable way to spend time (1)
3	Candidates should explain what the careers adviser's attitude was to sports journalism, and how one example of the writer's word choice makes this attitude clear. Identification of attitude (1) Reference (1) plus appropriate comment (1)	3	Identification of attitude, e.g. dismissive, contemptuous, disrespectful, scornful (1) Possible answers include: ■ 'spluttered' (1) suggests she was taken aback, lost for words (1) ■ 'doubted' (1) suggests she didn't think it was a viable career (1) ■ list ('technology, video games, …') (1) suggests she thought there were many competing attractions (1) ■ 'host of other things' (1) suggests she thought there were many alternatives to an interest in sport (1)

Question	Expected response	Max. mark	Additional guidance
4	Candidates should explain how two examples of the writer's word choice demonstrate how fierce the competition is among TV channels. Reference (1) plus appropriate comment (1) × 2	4	■ 'drives' (1) suggests power, forcefulness (1) ■ 'jostle' (1) suggests fighting, squabbling, jockeying for position (1) ■ 'fever pitch' (1) suggests heightened, almost irrational activity (1) ■ 'war' (1) suggests outright conflict, fighting (1) ■ 'giants' (1) suggests the sheer size of the competing forces (1) ■ 'cut the legs' (1) suggests violence, desire to maim, damage (1) ■ 'Trojan horse' (1) suggests taking over by subterfuge, cunning/underhand way of winning (1)
5	Candidates should explain using their own words as far as possible four pieces of evidence the writer gives to show that the careers adviser was wrong about people's interest in sport. Any four of the points in the 'Additional guidance' column for 4 marks.	4	Glosses of: ■ 'proliferation in radio stations', e.g. rise in number of radio stations (1) ■ 'hundreds of podcasts and blogs', e.g. extensive personal comment on the internet (1) ■ 'sport has colonised them [new technologies]', e.g. sport has taken them over (1) ■ 'most prevalent theme on Twitter', e.g. the most common topic, most talked about subject (1) ■ 'what people want to watch on a growing list of devices', e.g. what people use all the new communication technology for (1) ■ 'vehicle to break the ice', e.g. a topic which can start off conversations, get to know someone, help people relax in social situations (1) ■ 'allows large sections of society to come together in a shared experience', e.g. it unites groups of people with common national or cultural backgrounds (1)
6	Candidates should explain in their own words the importance of the 'Victorian era' in changing attitudes to sport. Any two of the points in the 'Additional guidance' column for 2 marks.	2	Glosses of: ■ it sought to 'redefine sport's moral status', e.g. change the way people saw sport as being good or bad (1) ■ 'help young people to respect rules', e.g. encourage them to obey the regulations or procedures (1) ■ '[help young people to] develop character', e.g. improve their personality, help them grow as (moral) individuals (1) ■ 'spread throughout the empire', e.g. became a worldwide influence (1)

Question	Expected response	Max. mark	Additional guidance
7	Candidates should explain how two examples of the language used (such as word choice, sentence structure or imagery) demonstrate the writer's feelings about sport. Reference (1) plus appropriate comment (1) × 2	4	■ use of question ('But where next?') (1) suggests some uncertainty about the future (1) ■ 'bubble' (1) suggests he thought interest in sport might disappear suddenly (1) ■ 'tipping point' (1) suggests he felt/worried there might come a time when interest reached a high point and then declined (1) ■ 'infatuation' (1) suggests he thought the interest in sport was overdone (1) ■ balance of 'When I started ...' and 'Today ...' (1) shows he is comparing doubt then and confidence now (1) ■ 'cultural giant' (1) suggests he sees sport as something huge, dominating (1) ■ 'not a bubble' (1) is a direct rejection of his earlier worry (1) ■ 'permanent' (1) suggests confidence in its staying power (1) ■ balancing of '[instead of ...] aberration ... true anomaly' (1) confirms belief that sport is fundamentally important (1)
8	Candidates should explain in their own words three reasons why the writer refers to the Ancient Olympics to support his argument. Any three of the points in the 'Additional guidance' column for 3 marks.	3	■ it provides him with 'the long view', e.g. looking at it over many centuries, not just a hundred or so years (1) ■ Ancient Olympics went on for over 1,000 years, showing it was important for a long time (1) ■ they attracted audiences/onlookers from far and wide, showing the popularity of sport (1) ■ they were not stopped even by major issues such as war or disease (1) ■ people were enthusiastic about them (1)
9	Candidates should explain in their own words three reasons why, according to the writer, sport is important to us. Any three of the points in the 'Additional guidance' column for 3 marks.	3	Glosses of: ■ 'speaks to something permanent in the human psyche', e.g. relates to deep feelings/thoughts (1) ■ 'No amount of ... will eradicate this', e.g. it can't be removed/destroyed by anything external or changed (1) ■ 'except temporarily', e.g. if removed it will only be for a short time (1) ■ sports 'move and inspire us', e.g. they stimulate, arouse passions, make us feel good (1) ■ 'themes of competition ... and rivalry', e.g. the key ideas of conflict and challenge (1) ■ 'teamwork', e.g. sport encourages working together, co-operation (1) ■ 'escape the humdrum and ordinary', e.g. get away from the dull, boring, routine (1)

Paper 2: Critical Reading

Section 1 – Scottish Text – 20 marks

NB The final question (for 8 marks) on each text should be marked using the general instructions below. Text-specific guidance for each final question is given at the relevant point.

Candidates may choose to answer in **bullet points** in this final question, or write a number of linked statements. There is **no requirement** to write a 'mini-essay'.

Up to 2 marks can be achieved for identifying elements of **commonality** as identified in the question.

A further 2 marks can be achieved for **reference to the extract given**.

4 additional marks can be awarded for similar references to **at least one other text/part of the text** by the writer.

In practice this means:

Identification of commonality (2) (e.g. theme, central relationship, importance of setting, use of imagery, development in characterisation, use of personal experience, use of narrative style, or any other key element …)

from the extract:

1 × relevant reference to technique (1)

1 × appropriate comment (1)

OR

1 × relevant reference to idea (1)

1 × appropriate comment (1)

OR

1 × relevant reference to feature (1)

1 × appropriate comment (1)

OR

1 × relevant reference to text (1)

1 × appropriate comment (1)

(maximum of 2 marks only for discussion of extract)

from at **least one other text/part of the text:**

as above (× 2) for **up to 4 marks**

Text 1 – Drama – *Bold Girls* by Rona Munro

Question		Expected response	Max. mark	Additional guidance
1	a)	Candidates should show how Cassie's admiration for Nora is conveyed. Reference (1) Comment (1) × 2	4	Possible answers include: ■ 'She was something' (1) shows she is in awe, giving high praise (1) ■ compares her with the Incredible Hulk (1) suggesting enormous strength, unstoppable when roused, on the side of right (1) ■ 'lioness' (1) suggests power, strength, nobility (1) ■ repeated words/single sentence 'She was.' (1) emphatic (1)
	b)	Candidates should explain how the dramatist conveys the liveliness of the dialogue in these lines. Each point (1)	2	Possible answers include: ■ frequent breaking into others' speeches shows keenness to add detail (1) ■ the way most of the interruptions are ignored, no malice detected (1) ■ Nora's replication of Cassie's exact words/tone shows the excitement in her voice (1) ■ Cassie's exaggerated, self-mocking description of herself ('one hand …') (1)
2		Candidates should explain one way in which the language conveys how fast-moving the incident was. Reference (1) Comment (1) Reference could be to word choice, sentence structure, tone, etc.	2	Possible answers include: ■ 'marched back up' (1) suggests speedy, purposeful movement (1) ■ 'here they were' (1) suggests coming upon them suddenly, unexpectedly; suggests how imposing, menacing they were (1) ■ 'dragging' (1) suggests hurried action (1) ■ 'without even a pair of shoes' (1) indicates he was not given any time to get ready (1) ■ the contrast with 'snoring … toasting … pie … can' (1) emphasises the sudden intrusion (1) ■ repetition of 'and' (1) creates a list-like sentence emphasising how much was going on all at the same time (1) ■ 'throwing everything every which way' (1) suggests frantic, panicky activity (1) ■ 'all over the house' (1) suggests widespread activity (1) ■ 'baby's screaming … child's calling' (1) suggests idea of everything happening at once (1)

Question		Expected response	Max. mark	Additional guidance
3		Candidates should explain how the dramatist creates humour in the way Cassie and Nora recall the event. Well-made point, i.e. reference + explanation (2) × 2 or Basic point, i.e. reference alone or weak explanation (1) × 4	4	Possible answers include: ■ Joe keeping his hand on the pie (1) seems bizarre in the circumstances of an arrest (1) ■ the idea of Nora singling out the biggest RUC man (1) puts her in an amusing light as the battling little woman (1) ■ the 'mountain/beetle' comparison (1) is greatly exaggerated for comic effect (1) ■ Cassie's 'Can you beat it, Marie?' (1) invites us to see the absurdity of the confrontation (1) ■ Nora's use of 'bastard' (1) after complaining moments earlier about Cassie's language (1) ■ the suddenness of the soldier's response ('Wallop') (1) given Nora's challenge not to strike a woman (1) ■ 'straight through the hedge' (1) suggests amusing, cartoon-like image (1) ■ Nora's self-deprecating 'Sure I got my answer …' (2) ■ 'Choked on her false teeth' might be literally true, but has humour in the indignity of mentioning such an item (2) ■ 'Mummy in the hedge with her little legs waving in the air' (1) suggests loss of dignity (after her previous self-confidence) (1) ■ 'oh but that was a terrible night' (1) said while crying with laughter is amusing in itself (1)
4		Candidates should show how the women's lives are affected by 'The Troubles'. Reference could be made to the following: ■ the death of Michael ■ imprisonment of Joe (and Davey and Martin) ■ taken to wedding in an armoured car ■ disruption to daily lives by road blocks, searches, raids ■ damage to bamboo suite by Army in pursuit of suspect ■ frequent sounds of gunfire off-stage – little attention is paid by the women ■ the raid at the Club ■ the silence at the Club for a dead IRA man (a regular event)	8	Marks for this question should be allocated following the guidelines given at the start of these Marking Instructions.

Text 2 – Drama – *Sailmaker* by Alan Spence

Question	Expected response	Max. mark	Additional guidance
5	Candidates should identify four ways by which the dramatist makes it clear that Alec is annoyed with his father. Four points from the Additional guidance column for 1 mark each.	4	Possible answers include: ■ says as little as possible/doesn't elaborate on anything he says (1) ■ doesn't look up when father speaks (1) ■ one-word response 'Aye' (1) ■ minimal/monosyllabic response: 'A book' (1) ■ very clipped 'Got an exam next week' (1) ■ impatient response 'That's what ah said' (1) ■ has to force out his 'Thanks' for the crisps and Irn Bru (1) ■ unmoved by his father's attempt to cheer him up by singing (1) ■ dismissive, slightly aggressive 'Chuck it will ye!' (1)
6	Candidates should explain how the way Davie speaks is typical of someone who is slightly drunk. Reference (1) Comment/Explanation (1) × 2	4	Possible answers include: ■ 'Och …' (1) suggests he can't think clearly enough to offer an explanation or doesn't think his son's concerns are important (1) ■ 'Just … wan a these things' (1) is a rather incoherent (or irresponsible) response (1) ■ the self-justification (1) of claims like 'Nae harm … Didnae even have a lot …' (1) ■ 'Wee refreshment' (1) typical, clichéd attempt to diminish the scale of what he's done (1) ■ enthusiastic recitation of Burns (1) is reminiscent of the poem itself (1) ■ 'Great stuff eh?' (1) trying to cajole a response from someone who's not interested (1) ■ the repetition of 'Reamin swats' (1) as if he's in a dream world (1) ■ 'Anythin for eatin?' (1) sudden change of subject suggests a rather confused mind (1)

Question	Expected response	Max. mark	Additional guidance
7	Candidates should show how the tension between Alec and his father is conveyed by the way they speak. Reference (1) Comment/Explanation (1) × 2	4	Possible answers include: ■ series of questions and short responses (1) indicates a less than friendly exchange (1) ■ the extreme brevity of Alec's responses (1) suggests he is unwilling to have any sort of conversation with his father (1) ■ the absence of any apology/contrition in Alec's responses (1) suggests he is quite content to offend/punish his father (1) ■ Alec's failure to respond to the promise of 'steak and chips' (1) suggests the depth of his antagonism (1) ■ Alec's reaction to Davie's mention of Peggy by banging down the book (1) shows he is angered/disgusted at his father's behaviour (1)
8	Candidates should show how they are led to believe whether or not Davie is a good parent. Candidates should discuss whether Davie is a good parent or not. They can argue for either side or for both. Reference could be made to the following: **Bad qualities:** ■ his drinking ■ his gambling ■ his irresponsibility with money ■ his constant 'something will turn up … we havnae died a winter' philosophy ■ his lack of drive/ambition **Good qualities:** ■ his obvious affection for his son ■ his support of his son's education ■ he tries to temper the sectarianism of Billy and Ian ■ he doesn't criticise Alec's religious phase, even though he seems to disapprove	8	Marks for this question should be allocated following the guidelines given at the start of these Marking Instructions.

Text 3 – Drama – *Tally's Blood* by Ann Marie Di Mambro

Question	Expected response	Max. mark	Additional guidance
9	Candidates should explain how the language used conveys Rosinella's hostility towards Lucia. Reference (1) Comment/explanation (1) × 2	4	Possible answers include: ■ the repeated use of 'eh?' (1) suggests impatience (1) ■ the two questions in first speech (1) both short, slightly aggressive (1) ■ 'I knew it' (1) as if she's outsmarted Lucia (1) ■ repetition of 'What's it say?'/'Read it.' (1) demanding, unforgiving tone (1) ■ use of imperatives (1) shows her as forceful (1)
10	Candidates should explain how the way Lucia speaks makes it clear she is making up a story on the spot. Reference (1) Comment/explanation (1) × 2	4	Possible answers include: ■ frequent ellipses (1) suggest pauses to think (1) ■ repetition of 'it just says' (1) suggests she's padding it out (1) ■ 'and eh' (1) suggests she can't think what to say next (1) ■ 'So he does ... and so do I ... as well ... I think so too' (1) empty words, flailing attempt to keep going (1) ■ 'No, it is good' (1) by deliberately misunderstanding Rosinella's comment she gets a chance to cause a distraction (1) ■ singing the song lyric (1) means she is relieved of the pressure to make anything up (1)
11	Candidates should explain how Rosinella's language makes clear her low opinion of Hughie. Reference (1) Comment/explanation (1) × 2	4	Possible answers include: ■ the use of 'that' in 'that Hughie Devlin' (1) sounds contemptuous, as if he were part of some lesser breed (1) ■ repeated pattern of 'I don't want you seeing him ... I don't want you talking to him ...' (1) suggests he is to be avoided at all costs (1) ■ refusal to engage in any of Lucia's defences of him (1) suggest she doesn't think he's worth discussing (1) ■ 'get rid of' (1) likens him almost to vermin to be eradicated (1) ■ 'Jumped up wee piece of nothing' (1) shows she thinks he is worthless and/or is getting above his station (1) ■ 'Him?' (1) reduces him to a sneering monosyllable (1) ■ 'the likes of him' (1) suggests she sees him as a type, not as a person (1)

Question		Expected response	Max. mark	Additional guidance
12		Candidates should show how the relationship between Lucia and Hughie develops. Reference could be made to the following: ■ initially 'forced' together to improve Lucia's English ■ at first, Lucia is a little disdainful of him/teases him ■ they become good 'play' friends (play at schools; blood brothers) though Lucia always has the upper hand ■ grow together naturally ■ Hughie is unable to express his love ■ gift of penknife; the hug ■ Hughie follows her to Italy ■ the 'Elopement' and happy ending	8	Marks for this question should be allocated following the guidelines given at the start of these Marking Instructions.

Text 1 – Prose – *The Cone-Gatherers* by Robin Jenkins

Question		Expected response	Max. mark	Additional guidance
13		Candidates should show how the writer's use of language creates a dramatic scene. Reference (1) Comment (1) × 2	4	Possible answers include: ■ the contrast between 'petrified' and 'leaping out' (1) creates a vivid picture of differing reactions (1) ■ 'petrified' (1) suggests absolute terror, shock (1) ■ 'leaping out' (1) suggests surprising, unexpected movement (1) ■ paradoxical/contradictory phrase 'berserk joy' (1) suggests confused, irrational, out of control (1) ■ short, blunt sentence 'There was a knife in his hand' (1) abruptly focuses attention on instrument of destruction (1) ■ colon after 'shouted to him' (1) introduces the disturbing detail that she didn't even know what she was shouting/that Duror was not in a state to hear her (1) ■ 'rushing upon ...' (1) suggests frantic, uncontrolled action (1) ■ 'furious force' (1) suggests frenzied, aggressive movement (1)

Question	Expected response	Max. mark	Additional guidance
			■ alliteration in 'furious force' (1) emphasises the ferocity of the attack (1) ■ 'savagely' (1) conveys the violence, brutality of the attack (1) ■ sequence of five short sentences from 'Blood ...' onwards (1) unelaborated to convey the stark horror, like a sequence of shocking photographs (1)
14	Candidates should explain in their own words what makes Duror's behaviour appear to be out of the ordinary. Each point (1) × 4	4	Possible answers include: ■ he stays on the ground with the dead deer (1) ■ he looks as if he's grieving over it (1) ■ he doesn't let go of the knife (1) ■ his speech is incoherent (1) ■ he keeps eyes closed (1) ■ he looks drunk (1) ■ his mouth is hanging open (1) ■ he appears like a simpleton (1)
15	Candidates should explain what impressions the writer creates of Lady Runcie-Campbell. Impression (1) Reference/explanation (1) × 2	4	Possible answers include: ■ accepts role of leader (1) 'came forward' (1) ■ can't help showing her disapproval (1) 'involuntary grimaces of distaste' (1) ■ tries to distance herself from anything unpleasant (1) 'avoided looking at the hunchback' (1) ■ concern for welfare of employees (1) 'Has he hurt himself?' (1) ■ rather detached, aloof (1) 'Has he hurt himself?'/refers to Duror in the third person (1) ■ formality of speech/ease of giving command (1) 'please be so good as to ...' (1) ■ expects others to jump to her command (1) saying 'Have we nothing to wipe his face with?' (1) ■ irritated by trivial detail (1) 'peevishly' (1)
16	Candidates should show how the writer creates a contrast between Calum and Duror. Reference could be made to the following: ■ essentially a contrast between good and evil ■ physically opposite: Calum is deformed; Duror is passed physically fit by Dr Matheson	8	Marks for this question should be allocated following the guidelines given at the start of these Marking Instructions.

Question		Expected response	Max. mark	Additional guidance
		■ emotionally opposite: Calum is caring, compassionate; Duror is vicious, destructive		
		■ psychologically opposite: Calum has child-like innocence; Duror has adult prejudices		
		■ Calum is always referred to by Christian name; Duror by his surname		
		■ Calum can't bring himself to kill the injured rabbit; Duror does it with ease		
		■ in Lendrick: Duror is isolated; Calum accepted by others		
		■ the echoes at the end of Calum as Christ (dead in the tree) and Duror as Judas (going off to kill himself)		

Text 2 – Prose – *The Testament of Gideon Mack* by James Robertson

Question		Expected response	Max. mark	Additional guidance
17		Candidates should show how the writer's language illustrates the idea that Gideon is in a 'crisis'. Reference (1) Comment (1) × 2	4	Possible answers include: ■ 'sweating' (1) suggests stress, pressure (1) ■ 'seething with energy' (1) suggests inner turmoil, hyperactive (1) ■ 'energy would burst out' (1) suggests dangerous eruption of activity (1) ■ 'wrecked' (1) suggests he would be in a drained, damaged state (1) ■ 'twitching' (1) suggests he is making involuntary movements (1) ■ 'as if in contact with an electric fence' (1) imagines some external force is controlling him (1) ■ contradiction of 'wanted to go … was afraid to go' (1) indicates the turmoil in his mind (1) ■ personification of the Stone (1) suggests irrational train of thought (1) ■ 'paced' (1) suggests agitated, stressed movement (1) ■ 'in and out … up and down' (1) structure suggests random, frenzied movement (1) ■ 'rushed to the front door' (1) suggests lack of control, desperate to speak to Elsie (1)

Question		Expected response	Max. mark	Additional guidance
18		Candidates should explain two impressions the reader is given of Lorna's character. Aspect of character (1) Reference/supporting evidence (1) × 2	4	Possible answers include: ■ brisk/no-nonsense person (1) gets straight to the point about her museum visit, no introductory chatter (1) ■ sensitive (1) notices Gideon's expression, asks if it's a bad time (1) ■ not easily put off (1) many possible references: e.g. talks over Gideon's attempt to speak, remains insistent about going to Black Jaws, gives several reasons for going to Black Jaws, etc. (1) ■ manipulative (1) looks 'pleadingly' at Gideon (1) ■ possibly capable of manic behaviour (1) 'I imagined her scraping and chapping at the windows' (1)
19		Candidates should show from that Gideon's thinking is both rational and irrational. Each point (1) × 4	4	Possible answers include: Rational: ■ makes a clear decision (1) ■ plans a definite course of action (1) ■ logical approach ('If ... then ...' formula) (1) ■ accepts that Elsie may be right/that he may need help (1) Irrational: ■ prepared to believe that the Stone could be influencing events (1) ■ prepared to believe in supernatural powers of the Stone (1) ■ something almost hysterical in 'confront them with the misery and mockery of our lives' (1)

Question		Expected response	Max. mark	Additional guidance
20		Candidates should show how the writer explores Gideon's relationships with women. Reference could be made to the following: ■ Jenny: quiet courtship (spurred on by Elsie); her attitude to Gideon's becoming a minster; marriage; contentedness; effect of her death ■ Elsie: early friendship in Edinburgh; admires her liveliness (finds Jenny more introspective); fantasises about her after Jenny's death; the sexual encounter; her belief that he needs help ■ Catherine Craigie: fascinated by her; drawn to her as a fellow non-conformist; admires her outspokenness ■ Lorna Sprott: a fellow eccentric; finds her irritating, but doesn't dislike her ■ mother: (when young) pities her because of how his father treats her; (when older) feelings about putting her in home, phones rather than visits ■ Amelia Wishaw: rather intimidated by her	8	Marks for this question should be allocated following the guidelines given at the start of these Marking Instructions.

Text 3 – Prose – *Kidnapped* by Robert Louis Stevenson

Question		Expected response	Max. mark	Additional guidance
21		Candidates should show how the writer's word choice emphasises how unpleasant the journey is. Reference (1) Comment (1) × 2	4	Possible answers include: ■ 'eerie' (1) suggests unworldly, scary (1) ■ 'buried' (1) suggests enveloped, cut off (1) ■ 'continually' (1) suggests relentless, non-stop (1) ■ 'blown and rained upon' (1) depicts them as victims (1) ■ 'drenching' (1) suggests soaking wet, completely sodden (1) ■ 'incessantly' (1) suggests relentless, persistent (1) ■ 'clambered' (1) suggests clumsy, difficult movement (1) ■ 'break-neck' (1) suggests dangerous, frightening (1) ■ 'rude' (1) suggests rough, harsh (1)
22		Candidates should show how the sentence structure helps to convey how David is feeling. Reference (1) Comment (1) × 2	4	Possible answers include: ■ first sentence: topic sentence (1) which introduces the idea of 'a dreadful time' (1) ■ second sentence ('I was ... his coat.') sheer length of sentence (1) conveys the enduring unpleasantness (1) ■ list of woes (1) suggests how many and varied they were (1) ■ repetitive structure of 'I was ... I was ... I had' (1) emphasises the personal nature of the suffering (1) ■ dash used (1) to introduce list of unhappy memories (1) ■ list of memories (1) shows how many there have been (1) ■ third sentence ('From such ... aloud.') list ('driving ... running ... enfolding ... falling suddenly apart') (1) suggests how all the elements are against them and/or dash used (1) for dramatic pause before an even more unpleasant feature (1)

Question		Expected response	Max. mark	Additional guidance
23		Candidates should choose one example of the writer's use of language and explain why they find it effective. Reference (1) Comment (1)	2	Possible answers include: ■ exaggeration of 'infinite' (1) not literally infinite but conveys the idea of huge number (1) ■ repetition of 'every' (1) emphasises that it is happening all around (1) ■ simile 'like a cistern' (1) suggests large quantity of water flowing from storage (1) ■ word choice 'filled and overflowed' (1) suggests ever-increasing abundance of water (1) ■ 'solemn' (1) [not current usage] suggests awe-inspiring, formidable (1) ■ the 'now … now …' structure (1) suggests the ever-changing nature of the sound (1) ■ simile 'booming like thunder' (1) suggests deep, loud, expansive, scary (1)
24		Candidates should describe in their own words the atmosphere between David and Alan. Basic point (1) More detailed description (2)	2	Possible answers include: ■ generally strained (1) extended silence, lack of communication (1) ■ David is reluctant to forgive Alan over their disagreement (over the money) (2) ■ the anger David feels towards Alan is making him angry with himself (2) ■ Alan's kindness and lack of anger are confusing/annoying David (2) ■ despite Alan's not showing resentment, David completely ignores him (2)
25		Candidates should show how Davie suffers a number of physical hardships throughout the novel. Reference could be made to the following: ■ at the House of Shaws ■ on board the Covenant ■ during the shipwreck ■ on the isle of Erraid ■ escaping after the death of the Red Fox ■ trapped on the rocks in Glencoe ■ illness and exhaustion before recovery at Cluny's Cage	8	Marks for this question should be allocated following the guidelines given at the start of these Marking Instructions.

There is further practical guidance on 'Kidnapped' in chapter 6 (pp.90–100) of *How to Pass National 5 English* by David Swinney (ISBN 9781444182095).

Text 4 – Prose – *The Telegram* by Iain Crichton Smith

Question		Expected response	Max. mark	Additional guidance
26		Candidates should explain briefly in their own words why the fat woman wanted 'to stand up and dance all round the kitchen', and why she did not do so. Each explanation (1) × 2	2	Possible answers include: ■ she wanted to: because (she is glad that) her son must be alive (1) ■ she didn't: out of respect for the thin woman/ didn't want to appear to gloat (1)
27	a)	Candidates should explain in their own words what it was the fat woman 'saw'. Each explanation (1) × 2 Award condensed answers.	2	Possible answers include: ■ how much the thin woman has suffered/ sacrificed to raise her son (1) ■ the extent of the thin woman's dedication to her son (1) ■ the extent of the thin woman's struggle to raise her son (1) ■ the extent of the thin woman's self-control/ restrained emotions (1)
	b)	Candidates should explain how two examples of the writer's use of language emphasise the impact it has on the fat woman.	4	Possible answers include: ■ repetition of 'she saw' (1) shows how many things she realised (1) ■ list of 'thin and unfed and pale' (1) shows she sees the extent of the thin woman's suffering (1) ■ 'so clearly' (1) emphasises the depth/clarity of her understanding (1) ■ 'astounded' (1) suggests how deeply shocked she was (1) ■ (imagery of) 'as if the air itself' (1) suggests something supernatural (1) ■ 'vision' (1) suggests something almost spiritual (1)
28		Candidates should explain two ways in which the language used creates a tense mood. Reference (1) Comment/explanation (1) × 2	4	Possible answers include: ■ the series/list of questions (1) suggests their uncertainty (1) ■ word choice of 'clutching' (1) shows the elder to be behaving oddly/in a heightened state (1) ■ 'like a man in a daze' (1) suggests they perceive him as behaving in a peculiar way/in a way they can't understand (1) ■ 'turning away from each other' (1) suggests strained atmosphere between them (1) ■ 'parted ... without speaking' (1) absence of normal civilities suggests something is out of the ordinary (1) ■ the fat woman's hesitation/uncertainty after leaving (1) suggests she is confused/nervous (1) ■ (relatively) short sentences throughout (1) suggests lack of engagement, basic details, staccato delivery (1)

Question		Expected response	Max. mark	Additional guidance
29		Candidates should show how Crichton Smith ends his stories in a surprising or thought-provoking way. Reference could be made to the following: ■ **'The Telegram':** tension unexpectedly relieved when elder passes both houses; twist at end when it is revealed that the telegram is for the elder himself ■ **'Mother and Son':** shock ending as son appears ready to attack/kill mother; made dramatic/enigmatic because story ends before any such act takes place ■ **'The Crater':** downbeat/sad/moving ending – soldier is dead after all their efforts; Robert's hallucination about comics; Sgt Smith's pragmatic thoughts ■ **'The Painter':** the painter is ostracised, then entirely forgotten once he leaves – rejection of the outsider/artist – narrator's final reflection on his own actions ■ **'The Red Door':** dramatic, 'cut-to-black' ending which leaves Murdo knocking on Mary's door, hearing his new red door saying 'Please let me live my own life'; reader can only speculate what happens; mysterious, but underlines key idea of Murdo taking control of his life ■ **'In Church':** shock ending when Colin is shot; irony of dying like this in the middle of a war; irony of dying in a church, at the hands of someone who decries war	8	Marks for this question should be allocated following the guidelines given at the start of these Marking Instructions.

Text 5 – Prose – *Virtual Pals* by Anne Donovan

Question		Expected response	Max. mark	Additional guidance
30		Candidates should offer two reasons why the writer has included the information at the start of each message. Each point (1)	2	Possible answers include: ■ to make them look like emails (1) ■ to clarify who is writing to whom (1) ■ to show that the reply comes within one day (1) ■ to create/sustain the illusion of these as genuine emails (1) ■ a wry reference to the idea that time on Jupiter (given to 100th of a second) is more precise (1)
31		Candidates should show how the writer creates a contrast in the girls' language. Aspect of language (1) Reference (1) × 2	4	Possible answers include: ■ Siobhan: chatty, informal, imperfect English (1): 'pure brilliant', 'all they big words', 'dead chuffed', 'gied' (1) ■ Irina: sophisticated, perfect English (1): 'delighted', 'confidences', 'somewhat concerned', 'substance', 'adolescent awakening of the sexual impulse', 'project their emerging energies' (1)
32		Candidates should explain in their own words as far as possible what differences there are in the girls' level of maturity. Aspect of difference (1) Reference/explanation (1) × 2	4	Possible answers include: ■ different interests (1) worried about gossip, not having pals; feminist thinking (1) ■ different level of intelligence (1) limited to simple issues; can understand complex issues (1) ■ different attitudes to education (1) very basic; has assimilated advanced concepts (1) ■ quality of expression (1) childish, limited; stylish, sophisticated (1)
33		Candidates should explain any one way in which these extracts are quite funny. Basic point (1) × 2 or Insightful point (2)	2	Possible answers include: ■ the 'joke' in the different timings, suggesting a more advanced civilisation (2) ■ the irony in using non-standard 'gonnae' in claim the exchanges will 'improve my English' (2) ■ the rather adult in-joke about the slovenly supply teacher (2) ■ the whole idea of messages from Jupiter (1) ■ the wise-beyond-her-years insight Irina has about gender politics (2)

Question		Expected response	Max. mark	Additional guidance
34		Candidates should show how the narrative technique helps to develop character and/or theme. Reference could be made to the following: ■ **'Virtual Pals':** imaginary exchange of emails between West of Scotland girl and a girl of the same age from Jupiter, allows light-hearted exploration of feminist themes and aspects of education ■ **'A Chitterin Bite':** alternates between two stages in narrator's life to reveal how she has developed emotionally and linguistically and how she has experienced abandonment in both ■ **'Dear Santa':** internal monologue style, reveals inner thoughts of narrator and her relationship with her mother, her feeling of being treated unfairly in relation to her sister ■ **'Away in a Manger':** third-person narrative from mother's point of view, allows reflection on her relationship with daughter and on the nature of Christmas celebrations ■ **'All that Glisters':** first-person narrative, allows for insight into narrator's personality and her relationship with her father ■ **'Zimmerobics':** first-person narrative by Miss Knight, allows insight (one-sided) into her relationship with her niece, and her becoming involved with the 'zimmerobics' class	8	Marks for this question should be allocated following the guidelines given at the start of these Marking Instructions.

Text 1 – Poetry – *Originally* by Carol Ann Duffy

Question	Expected response	Max. mark	Additional guidance
35	Candidates should summarise the key things that happen to the speaker of this poem. Each point (1) × 4	4	Possible answers include: ■ the speaker (and her family) move (1) ■ to a new home/country (1) ■ at first she feels out of place (1) ■ is treated badly by some of the locals (1) ■ is aware of her parents' worries (1) ■ eventually she assimilates (1) ■ by the end she is uncertain of her origins/where she came from (1)
36	Candidates should show how the poet's use of language makes a clear distinction between 'slow' and 'sudden' emigration. Reference (1) Comment/explanation (1) × 2 (i.e. once for 'slow' and once for 'sudden')	4	Possible answers include: Slow: ■ structure of 'leaving you standing, resigned, up an avenue' (1) creates a unhurried pace (1) ■ word choice of 'resigned' (1) suggests submissive, inactive (1) ■ 'no one you know' (1) suggests loneliness, isolation (1) Sudden: ■ structure of 'Others are sudden./Your accent wrong.' (1) sounds jerky, rushed (1) ■ structure of 'Your accent wrong' (1) very compressed/minor sentence like a sudden accusation (1) ■ sound/series of plosive consonants ('Corners … pebble-dashed estates, big boys') (1) creates harsh, rushed, slightly aggressive tone (1)
37	Candidates should show how the poet conveys the speaker's feelings of uncertainty. Reference (1) Comment/explanation (1) × 2	4	Possible answers include: ■ repetition of 'or' (1) shows she has no clear memory of when things changed (1) ■ series of questions (1) shows she is unsure/seeking answers (1) ■ 'only think' (1) suggests she knows it may not be the case (1) ■ list of things possibly lost ('a river …') (1) suggests there is a wide range of possibilities/she is unsure exactly what might have been lost (1) ■ word choice of 'hesitate' (1) conveys need to pause and think (1) ■ 'hesitate' placed crucially as the last word (1) emphasises her inability to answer a straight question (1)

Question	Expected response	Max. mark	Additional guidance
38	Candidates should show how Duffy creates a strong sense of character. Reference could be made to the following: ■ **'Originally':** character is nervous, has difficulty fitting in, is confused and uncertain ■ **'War Photographer':** character has undergone experiences which have affected his view of society ■ **'Havisham':** character has become twisted, vindictive, slightly mad ■ **'Anne Hathaway':** character expresses her deep enduring love ■ **'Mrs Midas':** character expresses her contempt for her husband, yet retains some feeling for him ■ **'Valentine':** character takes unconventional/cynical view of love	8	Marks for this question should be allocated following the guidelines given at the start of these Marking Instructions.

Text 2 – Poetry – *In the Snack-bar* by Edwin Morgan

Question	Expected response	Max. mark	Additional guidance
39	Candidates should summarise in their own words what happens in this part of the poem. Each point (1) × 4	4	Possible answers include: ■ the poet helps the old man wash his hands/ clean up (1) ■ they go back upstairs (slowly) (1) ■ (the poet watches as) the old man gets on a bus (1) ■ the poet reflects on how difficult life must be for the old man (1) ■ the poet expresses sympathy for the old man's plight (1)
40	Candidates should show how the poet makes effective use of repetition. Reference (1) Comment (1)	2	Possible answers include: ■ 'climbs … climbs … climb … climbs' (1) suggests the laborious, monotonous nature of the ascent (1) ■ 'And slowly we go up. And slowly we go up' (1) suggests the laborious, monotonous nature of the ascent, the dogged determination of old man and/or poet (and echoes earlier 'Slowly we go down …') (1)

Question		Expected response	Max. mark	Additional guidance
41		Candidates should explain what they think the poet means by either 'faltering, unfaltering' **or** 'endless, yet not endless'. Each comment (1)	2	Possible answers include: ■ 'faltering, unfaltering' is a contradiction/paradox (1) which suggests the old man's gait is inconsistent, or that what may appear to be hesitant actually has purpose (1) ■ 'endless, yet not endless' is a contradiction/paradox (1) which suggests that while the distance seems endless, it does in fact have an end point (1)
42		Candidates should how the poet's use of language creates sympathy for old man. Reference [1] Comment [1] × 2	4	Possible answers include: ■ 'Wherever (he could go)' (1) suggests poet is aware the old man will suffer indignities everywhere (1) ■ 'Wherever … dark' (1) suggests poet's sympathy for the perpetual blindness (1) ■ 'his most pitiful needs' (1) shows awareness that the old man's most basic needs will be made public (1) ■ 'in a public place' (1) shows sympathy for lack of privacy, for having to ask strangers, (slightly heightened by alliteration?) (1) ■ 'No one sees his face' (1) shows he is anonymous, not seen as human, individual (1) ■ 'Does he know how frightening he is' (1) shows sympathy for the fact that he probably doesn't realise the effect he has on people (1) ■ 'hands like wet leaves' (1) suggests sympathy for the man's weakness, frailty, unappealing appearance (1) ■ 'stuck to the half-white stick' (1) emphasises old man's dependence on his stick, sympathy compounded by idea that it is scuffed, dirty (1) ■ 'depends' (1) emphasises his reliance on others (1) ■ 'evade' (1) shows poet's awareness of how others shun, spurn the old man (1) ■ 'haul' (1) suggest sympathy for the effort needed (1) ■ 'blind hump' (1) is a very disturbing way to describe the old man's entire body, suggesting sympathy for the way his life is overwhelmed by his disabilities (1) ■ 'Dear Christ, to be born for this!' (1) final despairing cry, almost as if questioning why the man has been born at all (1)

Question		Expected response	Max. mark	Additional guidance
43		Candidates should show how Morgan uses language effectively to describe a character or a place or an event. Reference could be made to the following: ■ **'In the Snack-bar'**: character: the hunchback, poet/speaker; place: the Snack-bar, the toilet; event: the visit to the toilet, seeing him off on the bus ■ **'Good Friday'**: character: the drunk man; event: the 'conversation' between the poet/speaker and the drunk man ■ **'Trio'**: character: the three gift-bearers, the poet/speaker; place: Buchanan Street ■ **'Slate'**: character: the 'we' of the poem; place: natural landscape/Scotland itself; event: the birth of a nation ■ **'Hyena'**: character: the hyena; place: African jungle; event: hyena's speech of warning/self-justification ■ **'Winter'**: character: the poet/speaker; place: Bingham's Pond/West End of Glasgow; event: the coming and going of the ice on the pond	8	Marks for this question should be allocated following the guidelines given at the start of these Marking Instructions.

Text 3 – Poetry – *Assisi* by Norman MacCaig

Question		Expected response	Max. mark	Additional guidance
44		Candidates should explain how MacCaig creates a vivid impression of the dwarf. Technique/reference (1) Comment/explanation (1) × 2	4	Possible answers include: ■ word choice of 'hands on backwards' (1) suggests deformity, distortion, unable to function properly (1) ■ alliteration/sibilance in 'sat, slumped' (1) suggests lifeless, deflated ■ word choice of 'slumped' (1) suggests drooping, wilting (1)

Question		Expected response	Max. mark	Additional guidance
				■ imagery/simile 'like a half-filled sack' (1) suggests incomplete, lacking substance, inhuman, inferior material (1)
				■ alliteration in 'tiny twisted' (1) focuses attention, slightly harsh (1)
				■ word choice of 'tiny twisted' (1) emphasises the distortion, out of proportion (1)
				■ imagery of '(from which) sawdust (might run)' (1) suggests less than human, left-over material (1)
45		Candidates should explain how MacCaig's contempt for the tourists is conveyed. Reference (1) Comment/explanation (1) × 2	4	Possible answers include: ■ 'rush' (1) suggests they were not bothering to take much in, over-hasty (1) ■ 'clucking' (1) – compares them to hens, lacking individuality, not very bright (1) ■ onomatopoeic sound of 'clucking' (1) is mocking (1) ■ alliteration in 'clucking contentedly' (1) creates an imitative, slightly mocking effect (1) ■ 'contentedly' (1) suggests smugness (1) ■ 'fluttered' (1) suggests light, insubstantial (1) ■ 'passed' (1) suggests they ignored, discounted the dwarf (1)
46		Candidates should show how MacCaig conveys contrasting impressions of the dwarf. Reference (1) Comment/explanation (1) × 2 (i.e. once for 'superficial appearance'; once for 'inner beauty') Award condensed answers (e.g. on 'ruined temple').	4	Possible answers include: Superficial appearance: ■ 'ruined' (1) suggests crumbling, derelict (1) ■ 'pus' (1) associated with ill-health, infection, highly distasteful (1) ■ structure of 'eyes wept pus' (1) stark, monosyllabic description emphasises the horror (1) ■ sound of 'wept pus' (1) clash of sounds ('pt/p-') is very harsh, bitter (1) ■ enjambment in 'back … higher/than his head' (1) highlights the dislocation (1) ■ word choice of 'lopsided' (1) emphasises the distortion, visual difference (1) Inner beauty: ■ 'temple' (1) suggests a holy place, to be respected (1) ■ his voice is 'sweet' (1) suggesting delicate, pleasant (1) ■ he is compared with a 'child' (1) suggesting innocence (1) ■ he is compared with a 'bird' (1) suggesting natural beauty, freedom of movement (1) ■ he is compared with St Francis (1) suggesting piety, humility (1)

Question	Expected response	Max. mark	Additional guidance
47	Candidates should show how MacCaig creates feelings of sympathy in the reader. Reference could be made to the following: ■ **'Assisi':** enlists reader's sympathy for the dwarf; contempt for priest, tourists, Church ■ **'Aunt Julia':** enlists reader's sympathy for Aunt Julia's lifestyle; sympathy for speaker's failure to engage with her ■ **'Visiting Hour':** enlists reader's sympathy for both the speaker and the patient ■ **'Memorial':** enlists reader's sympathy at loss and grief ■ **'Basking Shark':** enlists reader's sympathy for the shock of the encounter, and with the subsequent reflections ■ **'Sounds of the Day':** enlists reader's sympathy for speaker's sense of shock, loss	8	Marks for this question should be allocated following the guidelines given at the start of these Marking Instructions.

There is further practical guidance on the poetry of Norman MacCaig in chapter 6 (pp.72–89) of *How to Pass National 5 English* by David Swinney (ISBN 9781444182095).

Text 4 – Poetry – *Keeping Orchids* by Jackie Kay

Question		Expected response	Max. mark	Additional guidance
48	a)	Candidates should identify four ways in which the speaker's behaviour makes it clear that the orchids are important to her. Each point (1) Textual reference not required.	4	Possible answers include: ■ she has kept them for twelve days (1) ■ she carried them with great care (1) (suggested by the simile 'like a baby in a shawl') (1) ■ she has them on display in her bedroom (1) ■ she takes care to restore them after they fall (1) … ■ … despite the odd circumstances of their falling (1)
	b)	Candidates should show how the poet's language conveys the idea that the orchids are a little mysterious. Reference (1) Comment (1) × 2	4	Possible answers include: ■ 'remain closed as secrets' (1) suggests they are hiding something, that she can't see what they're really like (1) ■ 'unprovoked' (1) indicates that the carafe has fallen over for no reason (1) ■ 'All the broken waters …' (1) can't be literal, makes a reference to childbirth, as if orchids somehow represent the relationship between her and the mother (1) ■ 'the upset orchids' (1) double meaning: they have literally been knocked over, but there is a hint of trouble/disturbance in the relationship (1) ■ 'with troubled hands' (1) suggests the poet's unease (1) ■ 'the closed ones did not open out' (1) some of them remained inaccessible, won't reveal themselves (1) ■ 'shut like an eye in the dark' (1) doubly inaccessible, refusing to give up their secrets, enigmatic (1) ■ 'the closed lid' (1) continues the figurative use of 'eye', suggests something cut off, kept secret (1)

Question	Expected response	Max. mark	Additional guidance
49	Candidates should show how the poet's language emphasises the difficulty the speaker has remembering her mother. Reference (1) Comment (1) × 2	4	Possible answers include: ■ 'are all I have' (1) suggests she has lost recollection of everything else (1) ■ 'fading' (1) suggests something disappearing, losing definition (1) ■ alliteration in 'face is fading fast' (1) emphasises the speed (1) ■ 'rushes' (1) emphasises the speed at which the memory of the voice is fading (1) ■ enjambment in 'rushes/through' (1) mimics the separation, dislocation (1) ■ 'tunnel' (1) suggests darkness, loss of vision/memory (1) ■ 'the other way from home' (1) suggests distance, opposite direction, loss of contact (1) ■ 'try to remember' (1) suggests it is hard, demanding, memories of the mother are vague, require effort (1) ■ 'scarf … brooch … coat … watch' (1) all she can remember are objects, nothing of the mother's humanity remains (1)
50	Candidates should show how Kay explores characters who are lonely or isolated or frustrated. Reference could be made to the following: ■ **'Keeping Orchids':** all three can be seen in the relationship between the poet/speaker and her mother ■ **'Bed':** the speaker is isolated (in the hospital and in the bed) and frustrated at her situation ■ **'My Grandmother's Houses':** the grandmother is lonely and isolated (especially in the high rise) ■ **'Lucozade':** the mother is frustrated at her treatment in the hospital; also isolated in the hospital bed ■ **'Divorce':** the poet/speaker is frustrated at her parents' treatment of her; feels isolated from the happiness she sees in other parent/child relationships ■ **'Gap Year':** poet/speaker is lonely without her son; a little frustrated at his devil-may-care attitude	8	Marks for this question should be allocated following the guidelines given at the start of these Marking Instructions.

Section 2 – Critical Essay

If minimum standards have been achieved, then the supplementary marking grid will allow you to place the work on a scale of marks out of 20.

Once an essay has been judged to have met minimum standards, it does not have to meet all the suggestions for it to fall into a band of marks. More typically, there will be a spectrum of strengths and weaknesses which span bands.

Marking Principles for the Critical Essay are as follows:

- The essay should first be read to establish whether it achieves relevance and the standards for technical accuracy outlined in the supplementary marking grid.
- If minimum standards are not achieved, the maximum mark which can be awarded is 9.
- If minimum standards have been achieved, then the supplementary marking grid will allow you to place the work on a scale of marks out of 20.

NB Using the supplementary marking grid:

Bands are not grades. The five bands are designed primarily to assist with placing each candidate response at an appropriate point on a continuum of achievement. Assumptions about final grades or association of final grades with particular bands should not be allowed to influence objective assessment.

Supplementary marking grid

	20–18	17–14	13–10	9–5	4–0
The candidate demonstrates	■ a **high degree of familiarity** with the text as a whole ■ **very good understanding** of the central concerns of the text ■ a line of thought that is **consistently relevant** to the task	■ **familiarity** with the text as a whole ■ **good understanding** of the central concerns of the text ■ a line of thought that is **relevant** to the task	■ **some familiarity** with the text as a whole ■ **some understanding** of the central concerns of the text ■ a line of thought that is **mostly relevant** to the task	■ **familiarity with some aspects** of the text ■ **attempts** a line of thought **but this may lack relevance to the task**	Although such essays should be rare, in this category, the candidate's essay will demonstrate one or more of the following ■ it contains numerous errors in spelling/ grammar/ punctuation/ sentence construction/ paragraphing ■ knowledge and understanding of the text(s) are not used to answer the question ■ any analysis and evaluation attempted are unconvincing ■ the answer is simply too thin
Analysis of the text demonstrates	■ **thorough awareness** of the writer's techniques, through analysis, making **confident** use of critical terminology ■ **very detailed/thoughtful** explanation of stylistic devices supported by a **range of well-chosen** references and/or quotations	■ **sound awareness** of the writer's techniques through analysis, making **good use** of critical terminology ■ **detailed explanation** of stylistic devices supported by **appropriate** references and/or quotations	■ **an awareness** of the writer's techniques through analysis, making **some** use of critical terminology ■ explanation of stylistic devices supported by **some appropriate** references and/or quotations	■ **some awareness** of **the more obvious** stylistic techniques used by the writer ■ **description of some** stylistic devices followed by some reference and/or quotation	
Evaluation of the text is shown through	■ a **well-developed** commentary of what has been enjoyed/gained from the text(s), supported by a **range** of well-chosen references to its **relevant** features	■ a **reasonably developed** commentary of what has been enjoyed/gained from the text(s), supported by **appropriate** references to its **relevant** features	■ **some** commentary of what has been enjoyed/gained from the text(s), supported by **some appropriate** references to its **relevant** features	■ **brief** commentary of what has been enjoyed/gained from the text(s), followed by **brief** reference to its features	
The candidate	■ uses language to communicate a line of thought **very clearly** ■ uses spelling, grammar, sentence construction and punctuation which are **consistently** accurate ■ structures the essay **effectively to enhance** meaning/purpose ■ uses paragraphing which is **accurate and effective**	■ uses language to communicate a line of thought **clearly** ■ uses spelling, grammar, sentence construction and punctuation which are **mainly** accurate ■ structures the essay **very well** ■ uses paragraphing which is **accurate**	■ uses language to communicate a line of thought **at first reading** ■ uses spelling, grammar, sentence construction and punctuation which are **sufficiently** accurate ■ attempts to structure the essay **in an appropriate way** ■ uses paragraphing which is **sufficiently accurate**	■ uses language to communicate a line of thought which may be disorganised and/or difficult to follow ■ makes some errors in spelling/ grammar/sentence construction/ punctuation ■ has not structured the essay well ■ has made some errors in paragraphing	
In summary, the candidate's essay is	Thorough and precise	Very detailed and shows some insight	Fairly detailed and accurate	Lacks detail and relevance	Superficial and/or technically weak

Practice paper B

Paper 1: Reading for Understanding, Analysis and Evaluation

The real price of gold

Question	Expected response	Max. mark	Additional guidance
1	Candidates should explain in their own words four things that make Juan Apaza's working life harsh. Any four of the points in the 'Additional guidance' column for 4 marks.	4	■ it is extremely cold ■ he has to protect/drug himself against hunger and tiredness ■ it is dangerous ■ he is not paid in the normal way ■ his only pay is a few hours to collect rock for himself ■ there is usually very little value in the rocks he collects
2	Candidates should explain how two examples of the writer's word choice demonstrate how unpleasant La Rinconada has become. Reference (1) plus appropriate comment (1) × 2	4	■ 'squalid' (1) suggests it is dirty, unclean (1) ■ 'shantytown' (1) suggests it is a slum, ramshackle (1) ■ 'toxic waste' (1) suggests it is polluted (1) ■ 'lawlessness' (1) suggests chaotic, unruly, anarchic quality (1) ■ 'no-man's-land' (1) suggests a war-zone, absence of order (1) ■ 'teems' (1) suggests it is overcrowded (1) ■ 'schemers' (1) suggests devious, unscrupulous people (1) Also accept: ■ 'flocked' (1) suggests a disorganised rush to live there (1)

Question	Expected response	Max. mark	Additional guidance
3	Candidates should explain how the language used demonstrates that La Rinconada is 'a place of … contradictions'. There are two possible contradictions: remoteness vs pace of growth; beauty vs ugliness. Be aware of and award a mixed approach. Reference (1) plus appropriate comment (1) for one side of the contradiction. Reference (1) plus appropriate comment (1) for the other side of the contradiction.	4	Appearance: ■ 'glint' (1) suggests an appealing gleam, slightly romantic (1) ■ 'magnificent' (1) suggests beautiful, stately (1) ■ 'like a wedding veil' (1) suggests beauty, purity, splendour (1) whereas: ■ 'stench' (1) suggests overpowering smell (1) ■ 'garbage' (1) suggests rotting refuse (1) ■ 'dumped' (1) suggests casually, thoughtlessly discarded (1) ■ 'waste' (1) suggests refuse, litter (1) ■ 'clogs' (1) suggests blocking up, causing overflow (1) Pace: ■ 'remote' (1) suggest it is isolated, quiet (1) ■ 'inhospitable' (1) suggests a hostile, difficult environment (1) whereas: ■ 'furious pace' (1) suggests population is increasing rapidly (1)
4	Candidates should explain why the sentence 'The scene … gold rush' provides an appropriate link at this point in the passage. **NB** Marks can be gained without direct quotation from the link.	2	■ 'the scene' looks back (1) ■ '21st-century gold rush' looks forward (1) or ■ 'the scene' looks back (1) ■ to the description of La Rinconada (1) or ■ '21st-century gold rush' looks forward (1) ■ to details of modern gold mining (1) or ■ reference to the ideas in the text before the link (1) ■ reference to the ideas in the text after the link (1)

Question	Expected response	Max. mark	Additional guidance
5	Candidates should summarise, using their own words as far as possible, some of the points made about gold. Any five of the points in the 'Additional guidance' column for 5 marks. Be aware of and award condensed answers.	5	Glosses of: ■ 'tantalized and tormented the human imagination', e.g. enticed/haunted the way people think (1) ■ 'For thousands of years', e.g. the fascination has lasted for ages (1) ■ 'driven people to extremes', e.g. forced people to wild, extravagant measures (1) ■ 'fuelling wars and conquests', e.g. has caused military conflict between nations (1) ■ 'underpinning empires and currencies', e.g. it has supported countries and their monetary systems (1) ■ 'levelling mountains and forests', e.g. has caused environmental damage (1) ■ 'not vital to human existence', e.g. is not a necessary part of life (1) ■ 'relatively few practical uses', e.g. it doesn't have many uses in everyday life (1) ■ 'density', e.g. its bulk, solidity, strength (1) ■ 'imperishable shine', e.g. it never loses its lustre, glow (1) ■ 'most coveted commodities', e.g. it is widely desired, sought after (1) ■ 'transcendent symbol of beauty', e.g. it is a supreme, unmatched mark of attractiveness (1) ■ 'immortality', e.g. associated with everlasting life (1) ■ 'an almost mythological power', e.g. it is seen as having almost supernatural qualities (1)
6	Candidates should explain in their own words why it is difficult to mine gold today. Any three of the points in the 'Additional guidance' column for 3 marks.	3	■ the fact that it is very scarce ■ what is left has been mined intensively in recent years ■ all the worthwhile deposits are running out ■ the remaining sources contain only tiny amounts of gold ■ most remaining deposits are in almost inaccessible places ■ there is danger of environmental damage

Question	Expected response	Max. mark	Additional guidance
7	Candidates should explain how two examples of the language used demonstrate the destructive nature of gold mining. Reference (1) plus appropriate comment (1) × 2	4	■ 'armies' (1) suggests aggressive, hostile forces (1) ■ 'converging' (1) suggests an organised assault (1) ■ 'crude' (1) suggests lack of thought for the consequences (1) ■ 'armadas' (1) suggests a large, powerful attacking force (1) ■ 'supersize' (1) suggests unnecessarily big, no concern for impact on environment (1) ■ 'big-footprint' (1) suggests the negative impact on the environment (1) ■ the balance of 'At one end …' and 'At the other end …' (1) suggests the huge range of different ways the mines are causing damage (1)
8	Candidates should explain in their own words what the writer means by 'disparities of scale'. 1 mark for understanding of 'disparities' + 1 mark for understanding of 'scale'. Be aware of and award condensed answers.	2	■ 'disparities' the difference, contrast, discrepancy (1) ■ 'scale' the tiny amount of gold recovered from the vast amounts of rock and ore that have to be dug up (1)
9	Candidates should explain why the last paragraph provides an effective conclusion to the passage as a whole. Any two of the points in the 'Additional guidance' column for 2 marks.	2	■ it brings the reader back to Juan Apaza, whose story opened the passage (1) ■ returns to the idea of his 'lottery' style of payment (1) ■ emphasises the traditional, superstitious way of life he leads (1) ■ reminds the reader of how desire for gold drives people to extremes (1) ■ is a personal tale after more generalised details of mining companies, etc. (1) ■ creates sympathy for Juan Apaza (1)

Paper 2: Critical Reading

Section 1 – Scottish Text – 20 marks

NB The final question (for 8 marks) on each text should be marked using the general instructions below. Text-specific guidance for each final question is given at the relevant point.

Candidates may choose to answer in **bullet points** in this final question, or write a number of linked statements. There is **no requirement** to write a 'mini-essay'.

Up to 2 marks can be achieved for identifying elements of **commonality** as identified in the question.

A further 2 marks can be achieved for **reference to the extract given**.

4 additional marks can be awarded for similar references to **at least one other text/part of the text** by the writer.

In practice this means:

Identification of commonality (2) (e.g. theme, central relationship, importance of setting, use of imagery, development in characterisation, use of personal experience, use of narrative style, or any other key element ...)

from the extract:

1 × relevant reference to technique (1)

1 × appropriate comment (1)

OR

1 × relevant reference to idea (1)

1 × appropriate comment (1)

OR

1 × relevant reference to feature (1)

1 × appropriate comment (1)

OR

1 × relevant reference to text (1)

1 × appropriate comment (1)

(maximum of 2 marks only for discussion of extract)

from at **least one other text/part of the text:**

as above (× 2) for **up to 4 marks**

Text 1 – Drama – *Bold Girls* by Rona Munro

Question	Expected response	Max. mark	Additional guidance
1	Candidates should identify four ways in which Deirdre's behaviour makes her appear strange. Any four of the points in the 'Additional guidance' column for 4 marks.	4	Possible answers include: ■ the very fact of her intrusion into Marie's home (1) ■ she is generally uncommunicative (1) ■ she is generally ungrateful for shelter/food (1) ■ her blunt opening question/absence of any apology for intrusion (1) ■ her ignoring of Nora's remark (1) ■ when asked again, merely gestures (1) ■ her eventual response is surly, discourteous ('sullen') (1) ■ the blunt, monosyllabic 'Back of the school there.' (1) ■ the loud, aggressive repetition of 'Back of the school there.' (1) ■ 'nods' and 'shrugs' – basic gestures only (1) ■ no acknowledgement of/thanks for tea/biscuits (1) ■ method of eating ('furtively and ravenously') (1)
2	Candidates should describe the way each of the three older women treats Deirdre. Candidates should make for each of the three women a general comment about her treatment of Deirdre and support it with appropriate reference to (but not necessarily quotation from) the extract. Reference (1) + Comment (1) × 3	6	Possible answers include: Marie: ■ helpful, welcoming, kind (1) ■ reference to: invites her in/offers tea/doesn't ask questions (1) Nora: ■ inquisitive/a little suspicious/hostile (1) ■ reference to: asks (and repeats) questions about where she is from, what has happened to her (1) Cassie: ■ suspicious, fearful (1) ■ reference to: looks away when Deirdre catches her eye (1)
3	Candidates should show an understanding of what is happening at the moment when Marie asks Nora to turn up the sound on the TV.	2	Possible answers include: ■ as a distraction (1) from the tension/nervousness created by Deirdre's behaviour (1) ■ to drown out (1) any comment from Cassie or Nora (1)

Question	Expected response	Max. mark	Additional guidance
4	Candidates should show how the role of Deirdre is important in the play. Reference could be made to the following: ■ her dramatic role as 'a catalyst' ■ her association with violence (the knife) ■ her quest for the truth ■ the effects of her intrusion into Marie's life ■ the effects of her intrusion into Cassie's life ■ her role as victim	8	Marks for this question should be allocated following the guidelines given at the start of these Marking Instructions.

Text 2 – Drama – *Sailmaker* by Alan Spence

Question	Expected response	Max. mark	Additional guidance
5	Candidates should explain why Davie is having money problems. Any four points from the 'Additional guidance' column for 1 mark each.	4	Possible answers include: ■ he is not earning a lot from his job (1) ■ he is gambling heavily (1) ■ he has suffered a significant loss (1) ■ he backed a favourite which lost (1) ■ he is in debt to the bookie (1) ■ he is paying high interest/not paying off the original sum (1)
6	Candidates should explain what the audience learns about Billy. Aspect of character (1) × 2	2	Possible answers include: ■ generous (1) ■ caring (1) ■ knows his brother well (1) ■ persistent (1) ■ nosey/intrusive (1)
7	Candidates should explain why Davie laughs. Each point (1) × 2	2	Possible answers include: ■ he knows his brother is joking (1) ■ he realises brother is trying to relieve some tension (1) ■ he is amused at the fact his brother can bring his sectarianism into anything (1) ■ he realises that the bookie's religion is not relevant/not going to change anything (1)

Question	Expected response	Max. mark	Additional guidance
8	Candidates should explain how the dialogue shows clearly the difference in outlook between Davie and Billy. The key point is the contrast between Davie's steadfast optimism (1) and Billy's realistic/cynical view of life (1) Supporting references (1 + 1)	4	Possible answers include: ■ general point that a hopeful comment by Davie (1) is usually countered by a pessimistic/realistic putdown from his brother (1) ■ the scathing 'Whatever that is' (1) showing that Billy lacks Davie's faith (1) ■ the blunt assertions 'It's a mug's game'/'The punter canny win' (1) in response to Davie's rather feeble 'Things've got tae get better.' (1) ■ the frustrated 'Flingin it away!' (1) in response to Davie's dogged 'Got tae keep trying.' (1) ■ Billy's desire for positive action about the bookie is met with Davie's passivity (1) 'Ah knew his terms.' (1) ■ Davie's rather pathetic shoulder-shrugging (1) 'Whit a carry on, eh?' (1)
9	Candidates should show how the theme of money problems and ways to escape them is explored. Reference could be made to the following: ■ Davie's gambling ■ Davie's drinking ■ Billy's move to Aberdeen for work ■ exchanges between Alec and Ian about work prospects ■ the idea of education as a way to betterment ■ football (and sectarianism) as a diversion from poverty ■ religion as an 'escape' ■ specific details of Davie's and Alec's situation	8	Marks for this question should be allocated following the guidelines given at the start of these Marking Instructions.

Text 3 – Drama – *Tally's Blood* by Ann Marie Di Mambro

Question		Expected response	Max. mark	Additional guidance
10		Candidates should show how the playwright makes them aware of two aspects of Rosinella's character. Aspect of character (1) Reference/explanation (1)	4	Possible answers include: ■ love for/pride in Lucia (1) 'looks lovely so she does'/'lovely legs when she birrels about'/'eyes are all lit up' (1) ■ ambitious for Lucia (1) wants to marry her into a 'good' family (1) ■ traditional (1) determined to marry Lucia to an Italian (1) ■ self-centred (1) ignores Lucia's attempts to speak (1) ■ snobbish/class-conscious (1) looks up to/wants to impress the Palombos; looks down on others (the type who boast 'Ma lassie cleaned four chickens') (1) ■ fantasist/delusional (1) convinced Lucia is 'daft for' Silvio Palombo (1)
11	a)	Candidates should identify the two things that Rosinella admires about Italians and show how her use of language makes her admiration clear. Admired features (1 + 1) Use of language: Reference (1) Comment (1)	4	Possible answers include: Admired features: ■ their hard work (1) ■ their love of family (1) Language points: ■ capitals at 'WORK' (1) to emphasise its importance to them (1) ■ 'I don't know anybody ...' (1) excludes all other nationalities (1) ■ 'Nobody loves their families ...' (1) makes Italians unique (1)
	b)	Candidates should explain how Hughie's words and/or actions show that Rosinella is being prejudiced. Reference (1) Comment/explanation (1)	4	Possible answers include: ■ seeing him enter with 'pail and mop' (1) suggests he is a hard worker (1) ■ list of all he has achieved ('cleared ... mopped ... cleaned out') (1) tells us he has been working hard (1) ■ 'working like a Trojan' (1) shows him as an extremely hard worker (1) ■ Hughie declines offer of (favourite) food (1) because of a family obligation (1) ■ 'don't like my mammy left on her own' (1) shows he has consideration for his family (1)

Question		Expected response	Max. mark	Additional guidance
12		Candidates should show how the theme of prejudice is explored. Reference could be made to the following: ■ Rosinella's always positive comments about Italians – sees them as special, more attractive ■ Rosinella's usually negative comments about Scots – can't look after their children properly, allow their girls to go out unsupervised, have looser moral standards ■ Rosinella's prejudice against Bridget when she is dating Franco ■ Rosinella's disapproval of Hughie's courting of Lucia ■ the treatment of Massimo by the public at the outbreak of war when his shop is attacked ■ the treatment of the Italian people who were interned during the war ■ the school teacher's racist comments to Lucia	8	Marks for this question should be allocated following the guidelines given at the start of these Marking Instructions.

Text 1 – Prose – *The Cone-Gatherers* by Robin Jenkins

Question		Expected response	Max. mark	Additional guidance
13		Candidates should explain two ways in which the writer's use of language conveys the violence of the storm. Reference (1) Comment/explanation (1) × 2	4	Possible answers include: ■ 'flashed' (1) suggests sudden movement, frightening (1) ■ 'crashed' (1) suggests something loud, destructive (1) ■ 'shattered' (1) suggests completely broken by a single blow (1) ■ 'hurled' (1) suggests that in the brothers' minds the storm has potential to throw them viciously from the tree (1) ■ 'fragments' (1) bits of the tree have been reduced to tiny pieces (1) ■ 'terrified' (1) the storm has the power to frighten an inanimate object (1) ■ repetition of 'every' (1) emphasises dominance, power of the storm (1) ■ 'torn its roots' (1) tree seems to have been pulled apart (1)

Question	Expected response	Max. mark	Additional guidance
14	Candidates should show how the writer's word choice makes clear how impatient Neil is. Reference (1) Comment/explanation (1)	2	Possible answers include: ■ 'flung' (1) suggests a quick, careless movement (1) ■ 'snatched up' (1) suggests a quick, unthinking movement (1) ■ 'shouted' (1) suggests he is urging Calum to move (1) ■ 'gasped' (1) suggests rapid breathing, losing patience (1) ■ 'clutched' (1) suggests frantic holding on (1)
15	Candidates should summarise the key points in Neil's argument to persuade Calum to go to the beach hut. Each point (1) × 4	4	Possible answers include: ■ for the sake of his (Neil's) health (1) ■ for the sake of Calum's health (1) ■ to avoid danger of lightning (1) ■ the beach hut can be reached quickly (1) ■ not to be afraid of Lady Runcie-Campbell's possible anger (1) ■ they won't cause any damage to the hut (1) ■ no one will know they have been there (1)
16	Candidates should explain how the writer makes Calum seem childlike. Basic points (1) × 2 or Developed answer on a single point (2)	2	Possible answers include: ■ 'They'll get all wet, Neil.' (1) a rather pathetic statement of the obvious (1) ■ 'Aye, that's right' (1) he doesn't realise that Neil's repeating of these words is sarcastic (1) ■ he takes Neil's question about the sun literally (2) ■ murmurs his response as if frightened to disagree with Neil (2)
17	Candidates should show how the relationship between Calum and Neil is developed. Reference could be made to the following: ■ Neil's protectiveness (e.g. over deer drive, in the pub) ■ Calum's unquestioning dependence on Neil ■ Neil's sense of having sacrificed his independence for Calum ■ Neil's recognition of Calum's innocence/goodness ■ Calum's efforts to please Neil (e.g. gift of the pipe) ■ Neil's occasional frustration with his brother	8	Marks for this question should be allocated following the guidelines given at the start of these Marking Instructions.

Text 2 – Prose – *The Testament of Gideon Mack* by James Robertson

Question	Expected response	Max. mark	Additional guidance
18	Candidates should explain how the writer makes them aware of Gideon's nervousness when he hears his father. Reference (1) Comment/explanation (1) × 2	4	Possible answers include: ■ switches off the TV (1) even though he knows there is no point (1) ■ 'jumped to my feet' (1) sudden action implying nervousness (1) ■ 'a flush of shame and fury' (1) showing embarrassment and resentment (1) ■ futile action (1) of trying to protect the TV set (1) ■ 'bowed my head' (1) suggests he can't look his father in the face (1) ■ fixes eye on crack (1) trying to shut out the presence of his father (1) ■ 'mumbled' (1) suggests he is confused, in a panic (1)
19	Candidates should show how the language used conveys the aggressiveness of Gideon's father. Reference (1) Comment/explanation (1) × 2	4	Possible answers include: ■ use of italics (1) to convey forceful tone of voice (1) ■ rhetorical question (1) to express fury at disobedience (1) ■ hint of cutting sarcasm (1) in 'you have become very skilled at operating that thing' (1) ■ 'huge right hand descended on my neck' (1) suggests sense of monstrous threat (1) ■ 'thumb and fingers gripped' (1) conveys the tightness, painfulness of the action (1) ■ 'increased the pressure' (1) making it even worse (1) ■ 'thought my head would snap off' (1) no thought for Gideon's pain (1) ■ 'breathing was like that of some monstrous creature in its den' (1) the comparison dehumanises his father, makes him sound like a mythical destroyer (1) ■ 'If I squirmed … his grip tightened' (1) no mercy, prepared to inflict even greater pain (1) ■ 'he pushed me' (1) forceful, aggressive action (1) ■ 'had squeezed out of me' (1) suggests painful pressure (1)

Question	Expected response	Max. mark	Additional guidance
20	Candidates should show how the language used conveys the father's contempt for American culture. Reference (1) Comment/explanation (1) × 2	4	Possible answers include: ■ the way he says 'What … is … that?' (1) as if spitting out the words in disgust (1) ■ his refusal to call the programme by its correct name (1) preferring 'Bat … man' as if the words are disgusting (1) ■ 'whatever that means' (1) implying it might mean anything (1) ■ 'drivel' (1) suggests he thinks it's worthless, idiotic (1) ■ 'unutterable garbage' (1) he considers it to be like rubbish, indescribably useless (1) ■ repetition/alliteration in 'Garbage from the land of garbage.' (1) harsh consonant conveys anger, disgust (1) ■ 'land of garbage' (1) implying whole country is contaminated (1)
21	Candidates should show how the relationship between Gideon and his father is portrayed. Reference could be made to the following: ■ influence of a strict upbringing ■ effect on the young Gideon of being a son of the manse ■ attempts to please his father (running, reading literature, joining Church) ■ envy of his 'single-minded devotion' ■ the two key things Gideon learned: 'the beauty of austerity' and 'how to hold my own in conversation' ■ effect of father's illness ■ father's behaviour during Jenny's visit to Ochtermill ■ death of father and Gideon's decision to enter ministry	8	Marks for this question should be allocated following the guidelines given at the start of these Marking Instructions.

Text 3 – Prose – *Kidnapped* by Robert Louis Stevenson

Question	Expected response	Max. mark	Additional guidance
22	Candidates should explain why Alan thinks that 'James must have tint his wits'. Any two points for 1 mark each.	2	Possible answers include: ▪ James must have gone mad (1) ▪ showing so much light (1) ▪ will attract the Redcoats (1)
23	Candidates should explain what impression Alan is trying to create of David when he introduces him to James Stewart. Impression (1) Reference (1)	2	Possible answers include: ▪ that David is a man of status (1) 'gentleman', 'laird' (1) ▪ that David is important, notorious, mysterious (1) 'give his name the go-by' (1)
24	Candidates should explain in their own words the differing reactions of Alan and James to the 'accident'. Each point (1) × 4 Maximum of 3 for one character.	4	Possible answers include: Alan: ▪ not bothered (1) ▪ attitude of win-some-lose-some (1) ▪ pleased that the Red Fox is dead (1) James: ▪ thinks it's bad news (1) ▪ with dire consequences (1) ▪ wishes Red Fox still alive (1) ▪ Appin will be blamed, will suffer (1) ▪ fears for his family (1)
25	Candidates should explain how the language used creates an atmosphere of panic. Reference (1) Comment (1) × 2	4	Possible answers include: ▪ list-like structure of sentence beginning 'Some were' (1) suggests extensive, frantic, disorderly activity (1) ▪ list of weapons ('guns, swords …') (1) suggests they are all lumped together (1) ▪ 'no kind of order' (1) indicates lack of a controlling hand (1) ▪ 'struggled together for the same gun' (1) shows unruly, disorganised behaviour (1) ▪ 'ran into each other' (1) almost cartoon-like disorder (1) ▪ 'continually turning about from his talk' (1) shows his lack of concentration, desperate to get some order into the men's activity (1) ▪ 'orders … never understood' (1) impression of futile activity, almost anarchic (1) ▪ 'anxious and angry' (1) clear signs of confusion and panic (1)

Question	Expected response	Max. mark	Additional guidance
26	Candidates should show how the writer presents the character of Alan Breck. Reference could be made to the following: <ul><li>his flamboyant appearance and behaviour</li><li>his bravery</li><li>his loyalty to his clan and his chief</li><li>his skill as a swordsman</li><li>his graciousness in defeat at the piping contest</li><li>his mentoring of David (e.g. in survival and in history/politics)</li><li>his fondness for David, despite David's Whig background</li></ul>	8	Marks for this question should be allocated following the guidelines given at the start of these Marking Instructions.

There is further practical guidance on 'Kidnapped' in chapter 6 (pp.90–100) of
How to Pass National 5 English by David Swinney (ISBN 9781444182095).

Text 4 – Prose – *Mother and Son* by Iain Crichton Smith

Question	Expected response	Max. mark	Additional guidance
27	Candidates should explain two ways the language used creates an unpleasant impression of the mother. Reference (1) Comment/explanation (1) × 2	4	Possible answers include: <ul><li>'mouth tightly shut' (1) suggests cruel, harsh, unbending (1)</li><li>'prim' (1) suggests strait-laced, prissy, moralising (1)</li><li>'anaemic' (1) suggests cold, pale, lifeless (1)</li><li>'bitter smile' (1) suggests hostile, nasty (1)</li><li>comparisons with insurance man (1) suggests smile is insincere, for show only (1)</li><li>comparison with 'witch' (1) suggests evil, wicked, power to harm (1)</li></ul>
28	Candidates should explain two impressions they are given of the son's character. Impression (1) Reference/explanation (1) × 2	4	Possible answers include: <ul><li>aggressive, spiteful (1) 'cursed vindictively' (1)</li><li>sense of hopelessness (1) 'helplessly' (1)</li><li>resentment (at loss of previous, better existence) (1) 'some state of innocence ... to which he could not return' (1)</li><li>something violent, destructive bubbling beneath the surface (1) 'still and dangerous' (1)</li><li>unemotional (1) 'answered dully' (1)</li><li>detached (1) 'He couldn't be said to speak the words: they fell away from him ...' (1)</li></ul>

Question	Expected response	Max. mark	Additional guidance
29	Candidates should show how the language used conveys the hostile atmosphere between mother and son. Reference (1) Comment/explanation (1) × 2	4	Possible answers include: <ul><li>exclamation mark (1) shows it's not a question but a criticism (1)</li><li>'snapped' (1) suggests sharp, aggressive tone (1)</li><li>'pettishly' (1) suggests petulant, irritable, almost childish (1)</li><li>'sitting there moping with ...' (1) direct criticism for neglecting his duties (1)</li><li>'don't know why we christened you' (1) insulting his very birth name (1)</li><li>'My father was never ...' (1) openly demeaning son with comparison (1)</li><li>repetition of 'All right, all right' (1) suggests irritable, bad-tempered mood (1)</li><li>'get a new record for your gramophone' (1) he's tired of hearing the same thing; insulting comment, comparing her to a machine (1)</li><li>the added 'hundreds of times' (1) emphasises how much it annoys him (1)</li><li>'she wasn't to be stopped' (1) shows her as relentless, persistent (1)</li><li>'mooning about the house' (1) suggests she sees his behaviour as pointless, childish (1)</li><li>'pacing up and down' (1) she sees him as distracted, acting strangely (1)</li><li>'taken to the asylum' (1) open allegation that he is not sane (1)</li><li>'something wrong with their heads' (1) insulting his father's family, shifting blame away from hers (1)</li><li>'in your family but not in ours' (1) insulting one side of the family, defending her own (1)</li></ul>

Question	Expected response	Max. mark	Additional guidance
30	Candidates should show how Crichton Smith explores conflict between characters. Reference could be made to the following: ■ **'Mother and Son':** conflict between mother and son ■ **'The Painter':** conflict between Red Roderick and his father-in-law; between the narrator and William; between William and the community ■ **'In Church':** conflict between Colin Macleod and the 'preacher' ■ **'The Telegram':** conflict between the two women ■ **'The Red Door':** conflict between Murdo and the community; between Murdo and Mary ■ **'The Crater':** conflict between Robert and Sgt Smith; between Robert and his men	8	Marks for this question should be allocated following the guidelines given at the start of these Marking Instructions.

Text 5 – Prose – *Away in a Manger* by Anne Donovan

Question	Expected response	Max. mark	Additional guidance
31	Candidates should explain how the writer's language creates a mood of excitement. Reference (1) Comment/explanation (1) × 2	4	Possible answers include: ■ 'shimmerin wi light' (1) suggests something alluring, attractive (1) ■ 'brightness sharp against the gloomy street' (1) the contrast emphasises the appeal of the square (1) ■ 'like the plastic jewellery sets wee lassies love' (1) suggests precious jewels, bright and shiny, children's enjoyment of play (1) ■ 'in a mad rhythm' (1) suggests something uncontrolled, zany, exhilarating (1) ■ 'ae their ain' (1) suggests the idea of freedom, individuality, lack of restraint (1) ■ 'bells ringin and snow fallin' (1) association with Christmas fun (and rhythmical pattern to heighten the sense of involvement) (1) ■ list of 'Reindeer and Santas, holly, ivy, robins ...' (1) emphasises the large number of attractions (1) ■ 'bleezin wi light' (1) as if on fire, extraordinarily bright (1) ■ 'fillin the air' (1) suggests the sound is pervasive, dominates the senses (1) ■ 'like a cracklin heavenly choir' (1) as if angels are present; suggestions of warmth, comfort (1)

Question		Expected response	Max. mark	Additional guidance
32	a)	Candidates should show how the writer's language conveys a vivid impression of people on the benches now. Reference (1) Comment/explanation (1)	2	Possible answers include: ■ 'huddled' (1) suggests bunched up against the cold (1) ■ 'auld coats' (1) suggests poverty (1) ■ 'sleep their way intae oblivion' (1) suggests desire to escape reality (1) ■ 'hauf-empty cans' (1) suggests attraction to alcohol or need to conserve limited supplies (1) ■ 'starin' (1) suggests blankness, lack of activity (possibly aggressive) (1)
	b)	Candidates should show how the writer's language conveys a vivid impression of people on the benches in the past. Reference (1) Comment/explanation (1)	2	Possible answers include: ■ 'down-and-outs' (1) suggests extreme poverty, homelessness (1) ■ 'faces shrunk wi drink' (1) suggest the physical effects of alcohol (1) ■ 'neglect' (1) suggests lack of care for themselves (1) ■ 'an auld cap' (1) suggests poverty (1) ■ 'hauf-heartedly' (1) suggests lack of enthusiasm, dispirited (1)
33		Candidates should identify four ways in which the conversation is typical of one between an excited child and a parent. Any four of the points in the 'Additional guidance' column for 4 marks.	4	Possible answers include: ■ Amy tugging at mother's arm to attract attention (1) ■ Sandra's 'Whit song?' as if she's not been paying attention (1) ■ Sandra's 'Do you?' as if struggling to show some interest (1) ■ Amy's gushing detail about school and Mrs Anderson (1) ■ Sandra's very uninterested 'Oh.' (1) ■ Sandra's 'What's no your favourite?' – she hasn't been paying attention at all (1) ■ Amy initiates guessing game (1) ■ Sandra won't play along ('Don't know.') (1) ■ Amy's wheedling 'Guess, Mammy, you have tae guess.' (1) ■ Sandra joins in to keep the peace (because she knows that's how to get it over with) (1) ■ Amy quickly resorts to 'Gie in?' (1) ■ Sandra accepts with alacrity (1) ■ Amy's triumphant 'Ah've won!' ... (1) ■ ... followed almost without a break by a question demanding an explanation (1)

Question	Expected response	Max. mark	Additional guidance
34	Candidates should show how the theme of parent/child relationships is developed in the extract and in at least one other story by Anne Donovan. Reference could be made to the following: <ul><li>**'Away in a Manger':** Sandra and Amy – mother trying to treat her daughter; daughter full of enthusiasm, wants to take homeless man home; mother rejects this idea</li><li>**'Dear Santa':** Alison's belief that she isn't loved; mother's behaviour appears to support this</li><li>**'All That Glisters':** narrator's loving relationship with father; her 'tribute' to him at the funeral</li><li>**'A Chitterin Bite':** relationship between narrator when young and her mother</li><li>**'Virtual Pals':** very adult, mature relationship between Irina and her mother – contrasts with lack of parental influence in Siobhan's life</li><li>**'Zimmerobics':** there is an element of parent/child in the relationship between Miss Knight and Catherine</li></ul>	8	Marks for this question should be allocated following the guidelines given at the start of these Marking Instructions.

Text 1 – Poetry – *Anne Hathaway* by Carol Ann Duffy

Question	Expected response	Max. mark	Additional guidance
35	Candidates should show how a sense of joy and happiness is conveyed. Reference (1) Comment/explanation (1) × 2	4	Possible answers include: <ul><li>'a spinning world' (1) suggests speed, exhilaration (1)</li><li>'castles' (1) suggests fairy-tale romance, luxury, security (1)</li><li>'torchlight' (1) suggests carnival atmosphere, brightness or restrained romantic setting (1)</li><li>'clifftops' (1) suggests dizzy height, dominance, distant horizons (1)</li><li>list of 'forests, castles, torchlight, clifftops, seas' (1) suggests profusion of exciting features (1)</li><li>'dive for pearls' (1) suggests romantic, exotic (1)</li></ul>

Question	Expected response	Max. mark	Additional guidance
36	Candidates should explain in detail how references to writing poetry and plays add to their understanding of the speaker's feelings. Reference (1) Comment/explanation (1) × 2	4	Possible answers include: ■ 'words were shooting stars' (1) suggests brightness, speed, exhilaration, mystical (1) ■ 'rhyme' (1) suggesting the lovers' connectedness, sense of belonging together, fulfilling each other (1) ■ 'assonance' (1) suggesting they are similar, connected, but retaining some individuality (1) ■ 'verb dancing in the centre of a noun' (1) suggesting her lover's ability to bring life, movement, action ... [this is a complex image which allows many analyses] (1) ■ 'he'd written me' (1) as if she is his creation, she owes everything to him (1) ■ 'a page beneath his writer's hands' (1) suggests she is a passive recipient of his creativity (1)
37	Candidates should show how the poet's language makes clear how different the guests are from the speaker and her lover. Reference (1) Comment/explanation (1) × 2	4	Possible answers include: ■ 'dozed' (1) sleeping (with a suggestion of indolence), while the others are more energetically and pleasurably engaged (1) ■ 'dribbling' (1) connotations of old age and messiness compared with the others' apparent vitality and clarity of purpose (1) ■ 'prose' (1) suggests their lives are dull, ordinary, uninspired, unlike the imaginative 'poetry' of the others' love-making (1)
38	Candidates should show how Duffy explores the theme of love. Reference could be made to the following: ■ **'Anne Hathaway':** deep, sensual, committed love between speaker and her dead lover ■ **'Havisham':** obsessive love turning to hatred ■ **'Valentine':** love as dangerous, corrosive ■ **'Mrs Midas':** disruption to a once passionate relationship, ambiguous nature of relationship by end ■ **'Originally':** love of origins, homeland (?) ■ **'War Photographer':** love of job (?)	8	Marks for this question should be allocated following the guidelines given at the start of these Marking Instructions.

Text 2 – Poetry – *Hyena* by Edwin Morgan

Question	Expected response	Max. mark	Additional guidance
39	Candidates should show how the poet makes the hyena sound threatening. Reference (1) Comment (1) × 2	4	Possible answers include: ■ repetition of 'I am' (1) creates dogmatic, arrogant figure (1) ■ direct address to 'you' (1) creates sense of reader/listener being directly targeted (1) ■ alliteration of 'fierce without food' (1) focuses attention on the hyena's aggressive nature (1) ■ sibilance in 'eyes/screwed/slits/sun' (1) creates hissing, snake-like sound (1) ■ word choice of 'you must believe' (1) sounds dogmatic, overbearing (1)
40	Candidates should explain how the sentence structure enhances the poet's description of the hyena. Reference (1) Comment (1) × 2	4	Possible answers include: ■ the question 'What do you think of me?' (1) suggests a provocative, threatening tone (1) ■ the structure 'I have … I am … I sprawl' (1) suggests self-confident, dogmatic (1) ■ the list of verbs (1) suggests range of movements (1) ■ the simplicity of the sentences/statements (1) suggests the single-mindedness of the hyena (1) ■ brutal shortness/simple monosyllabic nature of final sentence (1) highlights the stark conclusion of the hyena's activities (1)
41	Candidates should explain how the poet's use of language conveys the harshness of the hyena's world. Reference (1) Comment (1) × 2	4	Possible answers include: ■ 'Do you like my song?' (1) creates a slightly menacing tone (1) ■ 'hard and cold' (1) makes the moon seem unwelcoming, hostile (1) ■ the common romantic associations of 'moon' (1) are reversed/subverted (1) ■ 'slave of darkness' (1) suggests evil, vampire-like (1) ■ 'stone walls and the mud walls' (1) suggests primitive, prison-like conditions (1) ■ 'ruined places' (1) suggests desolation, destruction (1) ■ 'sniff a broken drum' (1) imagery of destruction, something with a purpose now ruined (1) ■ 'I bristle' (1) as if prepared for hostile action (1) ■ use of 'howl' (1) conveys the reality of the 'song' as wild, aggressive (1) ■ 'howl my song to the moon' (1) suggests madness, lunacy (1) ■ final question (1) is almost taunting (1)

Question	Expected response	Max. mark	Additional guidance
42	Candidates should show how 'Hyena' is similar or is not similar to at least one other poem by Morgan. Reference could be made to the following: Similar: ■ Ideas: transforms a simple idea (describing a hyena) into a deeper reflection (man's relationship with nature); all other poems can be seen as doing something similar (e.g. 'Trio' moves from a simple sight to a reflection on religion; 'Snack-bar' from a simple incident to a reflection on the plight of the blind man) ■ Language: effective use of word choice, sentence structure, sound; there are countless examples in all the other poems Dissimilar: ■ Ideas: use of non-human persona; in other poems with first-person narration (e.g. 'Good Friday', 'Snack-bar') the poet himself narrates ■ Language: repetition of 'I' creates a self-centred, slightly threatening persona	8	Marks for this question should be allocated following the guidelines given at the start of these Marking Instructions.

Text 3 – Poetry – *Basking Shark* by Norman MacCaig

Question	Expected response	Max. mark	Additional guidance
43	Candidates should explain in their own words what the poet's encounter with the shark made him reflect on. Each point (1) × 2	2	Possible answers include: ■ he reflects on the primitive origins of all life … (1) ■ … including his own (1) ■ he reflects on whether he or the shark is a 'monster' (1) ■ he reflects on the nature of evolution (1) ■ he reflects on how the nature of creatures such as the shark can be misjudged (1)

Question	Expected response	Max. mark	Additional guidance
44	Candidates should explain one way the poet suggests the encounter was quite alarming. Reference (1) Comment/explanation (1)	2	Possible answers include: ■ 'stub' (1) idea of sudden, unexpected, painful action (1) ■ 'where none should be' (1) mysterious, unsettling (1) ■ 'slounge' (word choice) (1) the very strangeness of it creates tension (1) ■ 'slounge' (onomatopoeia) (1) a fairly unpleasant, threatening sound (1) ■ parenthetical 'too often' (1) emphasises unpleasantness, no desire to relive it (1)
45	Candidates should show how any one poetic technique in line 6 adds impact to the description of the shark. Technique/reference (1) Comment/explanation (1)	2	Possible answers include: ■ contrast: 'roomsized' and 'matchbox' (1) emphasises the disparity between size and intelligence (1) ■ alliteration: on 'm' and/or on 'b' (1) adds weight, power to the scale of the shark (1) ■ imagery/word choice: 'roomsized' (1) exaggerates the size of the shark/conveys its enormity (1) ■ imagery/word choice: 'matchbox' (1) conveys brain as something tiny, almost inconsequential (1)
46	Candidates should choose any two examples of the poet's use of language in lines 7–9 which they find effective and justify their choices in detail. Reference (1) Comment/explanation (1) × 2	4	Possible answers include: ■ 'shoggled' (1) unusual word choice/register, perhaps a little light-hearted for such a momentous event, perhaps suggests poet's detached stance (1) ■ 'this decadent townee' (1) self-mocking tone, aware of own lack of connection with nature (1) ■ 'Shook on a wrong branch of his family tree' (1) humorous take on the effect of the encounter, idea of making him aware of evolutionary ancestors, of the shallowness of town-dwelling sophistication (1)
47	Candidates should explain what impression the last stanza creates of the poet's feelings about the shark. Impression (1) Justification/reference (1)	2	Possible answers include: ■ he is confused/uncertain (1) use of the question (1) ■ he is unsettled/scared (1) 'made me grow pale' (1) ■ he is not too concerned/knows it's only momentary (1) 'twenty seconds' (1) ■ he is no longer concerned (1) poem closes with the shark disappearing (1)

Question	Expected response	Max. mark	Additional guidance
48	Candidates should show how **'Basking Shark'** is similar or is not similar to another poem or poems by MacCaig they have studied. The number of possible permutations is huge, but the following possibilities could be considered likely: Ideas: ▪ similar in the use of personal experience to prompt reflection (**all set poems**) ▪ similar in use of wry humour (e.g. the priest/tourists in **'Assisi'**) ▪ similar in seeing things in an unexpected/surprising way (e.g. the 'fang' in **'Visiting Hour'**, the hand in water idea in **'Sounds of the Day'**) ▪ dissimilar in that central reflection is on mankind as a whole – most others concern specific people ▪ dissimilar in the absence of reflection on loss which dominates several (**'Visiting Hour'**, **'Aunt Julia'**, **'Memorial'**) Language: ▪ similar use of onomatopoeia/alliteration: common in most (e.g. 'swish', 'tin-tacked' in **'Basking Shark'**; 'clatter came' in **'Sounds of the Day'**; 'tiny twisted' in **'Assisi'**) ▪ similar use of striking imagery, e.g. 'roomsized monster' in **'Basking Shark'**; 'She was buckets' in **'Aunt Julia'**; 'carousel of language' in **'Memorial'**) ▪ dissimilar verse form: **'Basking Shark'** is much more 'regular' in line length, rhyme; **other set poems** are all free verse ▪ the use of unusual, surprising words (e.g. 'slounge', 'shoggled') is perhaps more marked in **'Basking Shark'** than elsewhere	8	Marks for this question should be allocated following the guidelines given at the start of these Marking Instructions.

There is further practical guidance on the poetry of Norman MacCaig in chapter 6 (pp.72–89) of *How to Pass National 5 English* by David Swinney (ISBN 9781444182095).

Text 4 – Poetry – *Lucozade* by Jackie Kay

Question	Expected response	Max. mark	Additional guidance
49	Candidates should explain how the poet makes clear the mother's negative mood. Reference (1) Comment/explanation (1) × 2	4	Possible answers include: ■ use of 'Don't' (twice) (1) shows she is rejecting things (1) ■ 'only wilt and die' (1) shows she is pessimistic (1) ■ 'nods off'/'fades' (1) suggests lack of concentration, couldn't care less (1) ■ dismissive tone of 'Orange nostalgia, that's what that is' (1) suggests she has no interest in the drink (1) ■ 'whole day was a blur'/'a swarm of eyes' (1) suggests she has no confidence in the hospital system (1) ■ 'Those doctors with their white lies.' (1) suggests lack of trust in doctors (1) ■ scornful/cutting tone of 'Did you think you could cheer me up with a *Woman's Own*?' (1) shows willingness to be rude to daughter (1)
50	Candidates should show how the poet's use of language makes a clear contrast between 'grapes' and the 'luxury' the mother asks for. Reference (1) Comment/explanation (1) × 2 (i.e. once for 'grapes'; once for 'luxury')	4	Possible answers include: Grapes: ■ 'have no imagination' (1) they do not appeal to her, she has no interest in them (1) ■ 'they're just green' (1) she sees them as limited, dull, featureless (1) Luxury: ■ list structure of 'the big brandy ...' (1) suggests an excess of enjoyment (1) ■ the alliteration ('big brandy'/'generous gin') (1) suggests luxuriating in the sound of them (1) ■ references to taste (1) suggests pleasure, self-indulgence (1) ■ 'dirty big meringue' (1) suggests a kind of self-indulgent glee (1)

Question	Expected response	Max. mark	Additional guidance
51	Candidates should show how the poem ends on a positive note. Reference (1) Comment/explanation (1) × 2	4	Possible answers include: ■ 'clear her cupboard' (1) has a hint of a new start, getting rid of the unwanted (1) ■ 'bags full' (1) suggests a sense of a job well done (1) ■ 'wave with her flowers' (1) suggests a cheerful gesture (1) ■ 'My mother ... waves back' (1) gesture is reciprocated suggesting a sense of connection (1) ■ 'face is light and radiant' (1) she can see brightness, almost angelic light (1) ■ 'sheets billow and whirl' (1) sense of freshness, unrestrained movement (1) ■ 'She is beautiful' (1) a straightforward statement of affection (1) ■ 'the empty table is divine' (1) by clearing away all the unwanted things, she has made a simple table seem somehow holy (1) ■ 'singing an old song' (1) implies contentedness and connection with her mother (1)
52	Candidates should show how Jackie Kay explores the theme of relationships across generations. Reference could be made to the following: ■ **'Lucozade':** speaker coping with her mother's illness, remaining positive ■ **'Divorce':** speaker's rejection of her parents ■ **'Keeping Orchids':** speaker's relationship with birth mother ■ **'My Grandmother's Houses':** speaker's relationship with grandmother at different stages in her life ■ **'Bed':** speaker's relationship with her daughter ■ **'Gap Year':** speaker's relationship with her son	8	Marks for this question should be allocated following the guidelines given at the start of these Marking Instructions.

Section 2 – Critical Essay

If minimum standards have been achieved, then the supplementary marking grid will allow you to place the work on a scale of marks out of 20.

Once an essay has been judged to have met minimum standards, it does not have to meet all the suggestions for it to fall into a band of marks. More typically, there will be a spectrum of strengths and weaknesses which span bands.

Marking Principles for the Critical Essay are as follows:

■ The essay should first be read to establish whether it achieves relevance and the standards for technical accuracy outlined in the supplementary marking grid.

■ If minimum standards are not achieved, the maximum mark which can be awarded is 9.

■ If minimum standards have been achieved, then the supplementary marking grid will allow you to place the work on a scale of marks out of 20.

NB Using the supplementary marking grid:

Bands are not grades. The five bands are designed primarily to assist with placing each candidate response at an appropriate point on a continuum of achievement. Assumptions about final grades or association of final grades with particular bands should not be allowed to influence objective assessment.

Supplementary marking grid

	20–18	17–14	13–10	9–5	4–0
The candidate demonstrates	■ a **high degree of familiarity** with the text as a whole ■ **very good understanding** of the central concerns of the text ■ a line of thought that is **consistently relevant** to the task	■ **familiarity** with the text as a whole ■ **good understanding** of the central concerns of the text ■ a line of thought that is **relevant** to the task	■ **some familiarity** with the text as a whole ■ **some understanding** of the central concerns of the text ■ a line of thought that is **mostly relevant** to the task	■ **familiarity with some aspects** of the text ■ **attempts** a line of thought **but this may lack relevance to the task**	Although such essays should be rare, in this category, the candidate's essay will demonstrate one or more of the following ■ it contains numerous errors in spelling/grammar/punctuation/sentence construction/paragraphing ■ knowledge and understanding of the text(s) are not used to answer the question ■ any analysis and evaluation attempted are unconvincing ■ the answer is simply too thin
Analysis of the text demonstrates	■ **thorough awareness** of the writer's techniques, through analysis, making **confident use of** critical terminology ■ **very detailed/thoughtful** explanation of stylistic devices supported by a **range of well-chosen** references and/or quotations	■ **sound awareness** of the writer's techniques through analysis, making **good use of** critical terminology ■ **detailed explanation of** stylistic devices supported by **appropriate** references and/or quotations	■ **an awareness** of the writer's techniques through analysis, making **some use of** critical terminology ■ explanation of stylistic devices supported by **some appropriate** references and/or quotations	■ **some awareness of the more obvious** techniques used by the writer ■ **description of some** stylistic devices followed by some reference and/or quotation	
Evaluation of the text is shown through	■ a **well-developed** commentary of what has been enjoyed/gained from the text(s), supported by a **range** of well-chosen references to its **relevant** features	■ a **reasonably developed** commentary of what has been enjoyed/gained from the text(s), supported by **appropriate** references to its **relevant** features	■ **some** commentary of what has been enjoyed/gained from the text(s), supported by **some appropriate** references to its **relevant** features	■ **brief** commentary of what has been enjoyed/gained from the text(s), followed by **brief** reference to its features	
The candidate	■ uses language to communicate a line of thought **very clearly** ■ uses spelling, grammar, sentence construction and punctuation which are **consistently** accurate ■ structures the essay **effectively to enhance** meaning/purpose ■ uses paragraphing which is **accurate and effective**	■ uses language to communicate a line of thought **clearly** ■ uses spelling, grammar, sentence construction and punctuation which are **mainly** accurate ■ structures the essay **very well** ■ uses paragraphing which is **accurate**	■ uses language to communicate a line of thought at **first reading** ■ uses spelling, grammar, sentence construction and punctuation which are **sufficiently** accurate ■ attempts to structure the essay **in an appropriate way** ■ uses paragraphing which is **sufficiently accurate**	■ uses language to communicate a line of thought which may be disorganised and/or difficult to follow ■ makes some errors in spelling/grammar/sentence construction/punctuation ■ has not structured the essay well ■ has made some errors in paragraphing	
In summary, the candidate's essay is	Thorough and precise	Very detailed and shows some insight	Fairly detailed and accurate	Lacks detail and relevance	Superficial and/or technically weak

Practice paper C

Paper 1: Reading for Understanding, Analysis and Evaluation

Why didn't people smile in old photos?

Question	Expected response	Max. mark	Additional guidance
1	Candidates should explain in their own words two key points the writer is making about early photographic portraits. Each key point (1) × 2	2	■ the people in them are not smiling (1) ■ they all look very stern/grave/dejected/miserable (1)
2	Candidates should explain how the appearance of early photographs is made clear by referring to two examples of the writer's word choice. Reference (1) plus appropriate comment (1) × 2	4	■ 'severity' (1) suggests harsh, stern (1) ■ 'frozen' (1) suggests cold, unmoving, stiff (1) ■ 'glumness' (1) suggests sullen, moody, miserable (1) ■ 'melancholy' (1) suggests sad, glum, gloomy (1) ■ 'introspection' (1) suggests brooding, ominous (1) ■ 'tragic hero' (1) suggests doom, death, suffering (1)
3	Candidates should explain in their own words the two answers the writer gives to the question he asks in lines 12–13. Each explanation (1) × 2	2	Glosses of: ■ 'to keep still for the long exposure times', e.g. in those days it took quite a long time for film to expose, so they had to avoid moving for a while (1) ■ 'an aesthetic and emotional choice', e.g. it's something they chose to do because they felt that way **or** because that's the look they wanted to project (1)

Question	Expected response	Max. mark	Additional guidance
4	Candidates should summarise, using their own words as far as possible, the evidence the writer gives that 'People in the past were not necessarily more gloomy than we are'. Any five of the points in the 'Additional guidance' column for 5 marks. Be aware of and award condensed answers.	5	Glosses of: ▪ 'did not go around in a perpetual state of sorrow', e.g. they weren't by nature gloomy all the time (1) ▪ 'they might be forgiven for doing so', e.g. although they had good reason not to be happy (1) because of … ▪ … 'higher mortality rates … medicine that was puny', e.g. likely to die young (1) ▪ 'had a sense of humour even about the darkest aspects of their society', e.g. they could laugh at even rather grim things (1) ▪ joking reference to cholera in *Three Men in a Boat* (1) ▪ Chaucer still funny despite being written at time of plague (1) ▪ Jane Austen makes witty comments during period of war (1) ▪ 'Laughter and jollity … institutionalised', e.g. enjoyment/fun were built into the way of life (1) ▪ celebration of Christmas as a time of fun is contemporary with the invention of photography (1)
5	Candidates should explain why the paragraph in lines 35–37 provides an appropriate link at this point in the passage. **NB** Marks can be gained without direct quotation from the link.	2	▪ 'the severity' looks back (1) ▪ 'true answer' or 'attitudes to portraiture itself' looks forward (1) or ▪ 'the severity' looks back (1) ▪ to the description the early photographs (1) or ▪ 'true answer' or 'attitudes to portraiture itself' looks forward (1) ▪ to the explanation of why they adopted this look (1) or ▪ reference to the ideas in the text before the link (1) ▪ reference to the ideas in the text after the link (1)
6	Candidates should explain in their own words two similarities between early photographs and having a portrait painted, and two differences between them. Any two similarities + any two differences for 4 marks.	4	Similarities: ▪ it was a serious, important event (1) ▪ not something that happened every day (1) ▪ was expected to be a lasting record (1) ▪ there was little smiling in the portraits painted by famous artists of the past (1) Differences: ▪ it didn't cost as much (1) ▪ it didn't take so long (1) ▪ it was available to more people, was more democratic (1)

Question	Expected response	Max. mark	Additional guidance
7	Candidates should explain how two examples of the writer's word choice demonstrate his liking for old photographs. Reference (1) plus appropriate comment (1) × 2	4	■ 'introspection' (1) suggests the people in them are deep thinkers (1) ■ 'haunt' (1) suggests there is something mysteriously enticing, alluring about them (1) ■ 'seriousness' (1) suggests they are important, weighty, not trivial (1) ■ '(more) moving' (1) suggests they affect him emotionally (1) ■ 'grandeur' (1) suggests splendour, magnificence (1) ■ 'gravitas' (1) suggests seriousness, solemnity (1) ■ 'traditional' (1) suggests established, worth keeping, to be admired (1)
8	Candidates should explain how two examples of the language used demonstrate his dislike of modern photography. Reference (1) plus appropriate comment (1) × 2	4	■ positioning of 'Today' at start (1) emphasises intention to compare unfavourable attitude to modern photography with his liking of old photographs (1) ■ sound effect in 'so many smiling snaps' (1) creates slightly humorous, sarcastic tone (1) ■ 'snaps' (1) sounds unimportant, trivial (compared with 'portraiture') (1) ■ 'absurd' (1) suggests looking for anything worthwhile in these photos is stupid (1) ■ series of short sentences (from 'Photos ...' onwards) (1) suggests how simple, uncomplicated these ideas are (1) ■ 'smile, laugh and cavort' (1) list of behaviours shows how much stupidity is involved (1) ■ repetition of 'endless/endlessly' (1) emphasises how tedious this behaviour is (1) ■ use of slang 'selfie' (1) suggests contempt for the whole idea (1) ■ 'momentary' (1) suggests it is fleeting, unsubstantial, insincere (1) ■ 'performance' (1) suggests it's an act (1) ■ repetition of 'zero' (1) emphasises how meaningless it is (1) ■ 'disturbingly' (1) suggests he finds it rather alarming, unnerving (1) ■ 'throwaway' (1) emphasises its transience, lack of substance (1) ■ use of parenthesis (1) adds a light-hearted remark to make them sound even worse (1) ■ simplicity of 'just press delete' (1) emphasises how disposable these photographs are (1)

Question	Expected response	Max. mark	Additional guidance
9	Candidates should explain why the last paragraph provides an effective conclusion to the passage as a whole. Any three of the points in the 'Additional guidance' column for 3 marks.	3	■ continues praise of old photographs (1) ■ 'beautiful and haunting' makes them sound particularly appealing (1) ■ continues to be dismissive of modern photographs (1) ■ 'silly selfies' is particularly scathing (1) ■ repeats idea that in the past there was as much fun, enjoyment as today (1) ■ presents older subjects as more dignified ('no hysterical need') (1) ■ repeats idea that the subjects had serious thoughts on their minds (1) ■ sums up with clear comparison/contrast: 'grave realities'; 'inanely happy ... snaps' (1)

Paper 2: Critical Reading

Section 1 – Scottish Text – 20 marks

NB The final question (for 8 marks) on each text should be marked using the general instructions below. Text-specific guidance for each final question is given at the relevant point.

Candidates may choose to answer in **bullet points** in this final question, or write a number of linked statements. There is **no requirement** to write a 'mini-essay'.

Up to 2 marks can be achieved for identifying elements of **commonality** as identified in the question.

A further 2 marks can be achieved for **reference to the extract given**.

4 additional marks can be awarded for similar references to **at least one other text/part of the text** by the writer.

In practice this means:

Identification of commonality (2) (e.g. theme, central relationship, importance of setting, use of imagery, development in characterisation, use of personal experience, use of narrative style, or any other key element ...)

from the extract:

1 × relevant reference to technique (1)

1 × appropriate comment (1)

OR

1 × relevant reference to idea (1)

1 × appropriate comment (1)

OR

1 × relevant reference to feature (1)

1 × appropriate comment (1)

OR

1 × relevant reference to text (1)

1 × appropriate comment (1)

(maximum of 2 marks only for discussion of extract)

from at **least one other text/part of the text:**

as above (× 2) for **up to 4 marks**

Text 1 – Drama – *Bold Girls* by Rona Munro

Question	Expected response	Max. mark	Additional guidance
1	Candidates should show how the playwright contrasts the characters of Marie and Cassie through their language and their actions. Contrast (1) Reference(s) (1) × 2 Reward condensed answers.	4	Possible answers include: Contrasts: <ul><li>Cassie's extroversion versus Marie's shyness (1)</li><li>Cassie's confidence versus Marie's timidity (1)</li><li>Cassie's self-centredness versus Marie's obliging nature (1)</li><li>Cassie's exuberance versus Marie's diffidence (1)</li></ul>Reference could be made to any of the following to support any of the contrasts: Words: <ul><li>Marie: 'Well, maybe ...' (1)</li><li>Marie: the rather feeble meat pie joke – attempted humour (1)</li><li>Cassie: 'great diet' (1)</li><li>Cassie: 'really feel the benefit' (1)</li><li>Cassie: 'Let them.' (1)</li></ul>Actions: <ul><li>Marie: 'shuffling cautiously' (1)</li><li>Marie: 'glances round nervously' (1)</li><li>Cassie: 'beams, applauding' (1)</li></ul>
2	Candidates should explain how the dialogue reveals aspects of the relationship between Marie and Cassie. Valid aspect of the relationship (1) Quotation or reference (1) × 2	4	Possible answers include: <ul><li>Marie cares for/is concerned about Cassie (1) 'Cassie, what's wrong?'/'Have you had words?' (1)</li><li>Marie is supportive of Cassie (1) 'It'll be all right Cassie.'/'I'll just be across the road, I won't let you go crazy.' (1)</li><li>Cassie feels she can confide in Marie (1) 'I tell you Marie I can't stand the *smell* of him.' (1)</li><li>Cassie knows Marie is unshockable/knows she can exaggerate with her (1) 'I'm just bad, Marie, didn't you know?' (1)</li><li>there is a kind of unspoken understanding between them (1) '*Slowly Cassie smiles at her.*' (1)</li></ul>

Question	Expected response	Max. mark	Additional guidance
3	Candidates should show how Cassie reveals her attitude to Joe, referring closely to the language. Reference (1) Comment (1) × 2	4	Possible answers include: ■ the use of italics (1) to emphasise her disgust/contempt (1) ■ 'greasy' (1) suggests unhealthy, slimy (1) ■ 'grinning' (1) suggests leering, unpleasant (1) ■ 'beer bellied' (1) suggests self-indulgence, unpleasant, sloppy appearance (1) ■ 'winking away' (1) suggests lecherous, unsavoury (1) ■ 'wriggling' (1) makes him sound worm-like (1) ■ 'fat fingers' (1) suggests clumsy, unhealthy, distasteful (1) ■ 'like I'm a poke of chips' (1) he treats her as a commodity, something for his own gratification (1) ■ alliteration ('greasy, grinning', 'beer bellied', 'fat fingers') (1) harsh sounds emphasise her revulsion (1) ■ climactic structure of the last sentence (1) builds to the horror of 'my *bed*' (1)
4	Candidates should show how the playwright presents the relationship between Marie and Cassie. Reference could be made to the following: ■ friends/neighbours of long standing ■ contrast: Marie rather dull, reserved; Cassie more extrovert ■ Cassie encourages Marie to enjoy life ■ Marie is simultaneously attracted to and shocked at Cassie's outspokenness, unconventional behaviour ■ superficially open and trusting, but Cassie has a damaging secret ■ eventual betrayal when the truth is revealed	8	Marks for this question should be allocated following the guidelines given at the start of these Marking Instructions.

Text 2 – Drama – *Sailmaker* by Alan Spence

Question	Expected response	Max. mark	Additional guidance
5	Candidates should summarise what is said between Davie and Billy. 1 mark for each acceptable point × 4 Quotation is likely but not necessary.	4	Possible answers include: ■ Davie tells Billy he has lost his job (1) ■ Billy says it's not Davie's fault/not fair/criticises employers (1) ■ Davie is very defeatist/thinks he's got nothing going for him (1) ■ Billy says he might be able to get him a job (1) ■ Davie displays little enthusiasm (1) ■ Billy tries to keep Davie's spirits up (1)
6	Candidates should explain how the sentence structure helps the audience to understand how Davie is feeling. Reference to sentence structure (1) Comment (1)	2	Possible answers include: ■ exclamation (1) shows his feeling of hopelessness, defeat (1) ■ use of italics (1) shows how resentful he feels about 'them' (1) ■ series of short sentences (1) suggests he is disengaged, depressed, has given up (1) ■ series of questions (1) suggests he is at a loss, feels hopeless (1)
7	Candidates should explain how the dialogue emphasises the difference between Davie and Billy. Comment (1) × 2	2	Possible answers include: ■ Davie has very little to say/is monosyllabic/sounds defeated (1) ■ Billy talks at greater length/offers hope/encouragement (1)
8	Candidates should explain in detail what is revealed about Davie's personality. Comment (1) Reference (1) × 2	4	Possible answers include: ■ unambitious/never one to get excited (1) 'wouldnae be much' (1) ■ feels sort of powerless to affect anything (1) *'Shrugs'* (1) ■ takes life as it comes (1) 'better than nothing' (1) ■ keen to rationalise/make best of situation (1) 'that was a lousy job anyway' (1) ■ mild surprise at something trivial (1) 'Amazin how it gets on top of ye' (1) ■ resigned acceptance of everything (1) 'Ach aye. No to worry.' (1) ■ clichéd optimism (or possible ironic repetition of Billy earlier) (1) 'Never died a winter yet' (1)

Question	Expected response	Max. mark	Additional guidance
9	Candidates should show how the playwright presents the character of Davie. Reference could be made to the following: ■ self-pitying ■ lacking drive, ambition ■ takes refuge in drink ■ loves his son but doesn't really understand him ■ lives in the past ■ always hopes that things will improve, but is never very confident ■ passive, just lets life happen to him	8	Marks for this question should be allocated following the guidelines given at the start of these Marking Instructions.

Text 3 – Drama – *Tally's Blood* by Ann Marie Di Mambro

Question	Expected response	Max. mark	Additional guidance
10	Candidates should summarise what happens in the extract. Each point (1) × 3 Quotation is likely but not necessary.	3	Possible answers include: ■ Rosinella and Massimo argue (over Rosinella's spoiling of Lucia) (1) ■ Massimo admires Lucia's schoolbag (1) ■ Lucia refuse to take off her dress (1) ■ Massimo suggests a compromise (1) ■ the compromise works (1)
11	Candidates should identify two aspects of Rosinella's character. Each point (1) × 2 Quotation/reference is likely but not necessary.	2	Possible answers include: ■ she loves Lucia (1) ■ she is generous towards Lucia/is prepared to spoil her (1) ■ she is selfless/altruistic (1) ■ she is unashamed of her generosity (1)
12	Candidates should explain how the playwright makes Lucia's behaviour typical of a young child. Reference (1) Explanation (1) × 2	4	Possible answers include: ■ the stubbornness (1) implied by repetition (of 'No' and/or 'I want to keep it on') (1) ■ the quick change(s) of mood (1) from playful to petulant (1) ■ starting to shout (1) + example (1) ■ yielding to adult compromise (1) + example (1) ■ Accept also: perhaps she is aware all along that one of them will weaken … (1)

Question	Expected response	Max. mark	Additional guidance
13	Candidates should give examples of speech which shows clear signs of Scottish usage. Each example (1) × 3	3	Possible answers include: ■ 'see when I ...' (1) ■ 'wee' (1) ■ 'lassie' (1) ■ 'wean' (1) ■ 'no' (for 'not') (1) ■ 'tatties' (1) ■ 'hen' (1) ■ 'I says' (1)
14	Candidates should show how the relationship between Lucia and her aunt and uncle is portrayed. Reference could be made to the following: ■ Rosinella and Massimo's adoption of Lucia implies loving/caring ■ Rosinella's sacrifice to buy Lucia the dress ■ fairly typical parent–child relationship in early days: disagreements over school; use of swear word; Lucia plays one adult against the other ■ Lucia's 'dutiful niece' side – helps in shop, etc. ■ Lucia's resentment at Rosinella's match-making with Silvio Palombo ■ Rosinella and Massimo's disapproval of relationship with Hughie ■ eventual acceptance of it	8	Marks for this question should be allocated following the guidelines given at the start of these Marking Instructions.

Text 1 – Prose – *The Cone-Gatherers* by Robin Jenkins

Question	Expected response	Max. mark	Additional guidance
15	Candidates should summarise what happens in the extract. Each point (1) × 4	4	Possible answers include: ■ Duror is unable to climb tree (1) ■ Neil is initially polite (1) ■ Duror delivers message to Calum and Neil about the deer drive (1) ■ Neil protests strongly (1) ■ the effect on Duror of being unable to climb the tree is evident (1)

Question	Expected response	Max. mark	Additional guidance
16	Candidates should show how the writer creates a tense mood in the first two paragraphs. Reference (1) Comment/explanation (1)	2	Possible answers include: ■ 'scrapes'/'thumps'/'cracked'/'barked' (1) use of onomatopoeia to create threatening sounds (1) ■ the frequency of short sentences (1) creates a breathless, staccato effect (1) ■ the alternation between sound and silence (1) creates suspense (1) ■ the references to waiting, once for 'three or four minutes' (1) an agonisingly long time (1) ■ the barking of the dog (1) could be seen as intimidating (1)
17	Candidates should show how Neil's attitude to Duror goes through at least two changes. Each point (1) × 4 There should be reference to at least three attitudes in order to establish two changes. Textual reference is likely but not essential. Reward condensed answers.	4	Possible answers include: ■ initially friendly/polite ('It's a grand day, isn't it?') (1) ■ then helpful ('Do you want to talk to us about something?') (1) ■ sees Duror as possible bringer of good news ('Have we to go back home?') (1) ■ non-committal/defensive ('We know that.') (1) ■ angry/slightly aggressive ('How could he?'/ repeated 'Didn't he ...') (1) ■ disbelieving/indignant ('What's the good of all that ...') (1) ■ very assertive ('It's just a trick') (1)
18	Candidates should explain what the image in the last sentence of the extract tells them about Duror. Clear explanation (2) Weaker explanation (1)	2	Possible answers include: ■ on the outside he appears normal/healthy (1) but a malignant force is destroying him from within (1)
19	Candidates should show how the conflict between Duror and the cone-gatherers is explored. Reference could be made to the following: ■ his hatred for them from the outset ■ the irrational nature of his hatred ■ his silent vigil at their hut ■ the deer drive ■ his attempts to blacken their reputation ■ the incident in the pub ■ the climax of the novel	8	Marks for this question should be allocated following the guidelines given at the start of these Marking Instructions.

Text 2 – Prose – *The Testament of Gideon Mack* by James Robertson

Question	Expected response	Max. mark	Additional guidance
20	Candidates should show how the writer portrays Miss Craigie as an intimidating character. Reference (1) Comment/explanation (1) × 2	4	Possible answers include: ■ 'Just come in, for heaven's sake' (1) brusque, irritable, impatient (1) ■ '*If locked go away*' (1) the notice is unwelcoming, abrupt (1) ■ 'Can't you read?' (1) almost aggressive, demeaning (1) ■ undermines Gideon's attempt to be apologetic (1) with sarcastic response (1) ■ 'Oh, it's you.' (1) in a clearly unwelcoming tone (1) ■ 'distaste' (1) shows her disapproval of Gideon/of the Kirk (1) ■ her reputation as believing Kirk to be 'a scabrous outbreak …' (1) sees Kirk/religion as a disease, something that blights society (1)
21	Candidates should show how the dialogue conveys the friction between Gideon and Miss Craigie. Reference (1) Comment/explanation (1) × 2	4	Possible answers include: ■ general point: every one of Gideon's attempts at politeness (1) is turned against him by her curt responses (1) ■ her immediate contradiction (1) of what he says about the clerical collar (1) ■ her (logical but) rude response (1) when he says he's been reading her book and wants to ask some questions (1) ■ her (understandable but) unnecessary comment (1) about knowing what the word 'supplementary' means (1)
22	Candidates should show how the writer's sentence structure and imagery help to describe the layout of Miss Craigie's hallway. Reference (1) Comment/explanation (1) × 2 For full marks both features should be dealt with.	4	Possible answers include: Sentence structure: ■ the colon (after 'location') (1) introduces explanation of what he realises is the reason for the layout (1) ■ the colon (after 'placed') (1) introduces explanation of both the 'pre-existing' and the 'strategically placed' (1) ■ the list beginning 'plant-stand' (1) illustrates the large number of objects involved (1) **and/or** creates an imitation of the step-by-step nature of the arrangement (1) Imagery: ■ 'a kind of domestic rock-face' (1) just as a rock face can be climbed with the help of pre-planned places to grip, so there are objects positioned to help her negotiate the hallway (1) ■ 'horizontal climbing-wall' (1) just as a climbing wall is ascended vertically with artificial aids, so she can move along her hallway aided by these objects (1)

Question	Expected response	Max. mark	Additional guidance
23	Candidates should show how the character of Miss Craigie is important in *The Testament of Gideon Mack*. Reference could be made to the following: ■ like Gideon, she is an outsider viewed with suspicion by the community ■ her reputation as knowledgeable about the area ■ Gideon's fascination with/ attraction to her ■ her unashamed agnosticism ■ her attitude to alcohol and soft drugs ■ her contempt for Winnyford ■ her instructions for her funeral	8	Marks for this question should be allocated following the guidelines given at the start of these Marking Instructions.

Text 3 – Prose – *Kidnapped* by Robert Louis Stevenson

Question	Expected response	Max. mark	Additional guidance
24	Candidates should identify briefly two different emotions David feels. Emotion (1) × 2 No reference/quotation required.	2	Possible answers include: ■ uncertainty (1) ■ fear (1) ■ hopelessness (1) ■ anger (1) ■ a desire for it to be over (1)
25	Candidates should explain two ways by which the writer makes the events dramatic and exciting. Reference (1) Comment (1) × 2	4	Possible answers include: ■ 'all of a sudden' (1) surprise, frightening (1) ■ 'a rush of feet' (1) speed, threat (1) ■ 'a roar' (1) loud, aggressive sound (1) ■ 'and … and … and' (1) structure (list form) gives impression of one action following quickly after another (1) ■ 'some one crying out as if hurt' (1) uncertainty (1) ■ 'I cried' (1) the exclamation shows his state of alarm (1) ■ 'Look to your window!' (1) Alan's exclamation draws attention to more danger (1) ■ 'pass his sword through the mate's body' (1) gruesome killing (1) ■ 'drive the door in' (1) idea of force, threat (1) ■ 'But it was now or never' (1) idea of last chance, resolved to his fate (1) ■ 'shot into their midst' (1) reckless, desperate action (1) ■ 'the whole party threw down the yard and ran for it' (1) sense of victory (1)

Question	Expected response	Max. mark	Additional guidance
26	Candidates should explain two impressions they are given of Alan Breck's personality. Aspect of personality (1) Reference (1) × 2	4	Possible answers include: ■ bloodthirsty (1) 'his sword was running blood to the hilt' (1) ■ proud (1) 'himself so swelled with triumph' (1) ■ impressive appearance (1) 'looked to be invincible' (1) ■ believer in cause/contempt for opponents (1) 'There's one of your Whigs for ye!' (1) ■ callous (1) 'asked if I had done much execution' (1)
27	Candidates should explain what Alan means by 'This was but a dram before meat.' Clear explanation (2) Basic explanation (1)	2	Possible answers include: ■ what they've experienced so far is nothing much ('but a dram') (1) ■ much worse, a more substantial battle is yet to come ('meat') (1)
28	Candidates should show how the relationship between David and Alan Breck develops. Reference could be made to the following: ■ the contrasting natures of the characters as developed throughout the novel ■ tensions in the relationship as it develops throughout the novel ■ the theme of duality established by looking at the relationship throughout the novel ■ the admiration the characters have for each other at points throughout the novel ■ the developing movement from uncertainty towards true friendship and understanding which is developed throughout the novel ■ a mixture of elements from some or all of the above	8	Marks for this question should be allocated following the guidelines given at the start of these Marking Instructions.

There is further practical guidance on 'Kidnapped' in chapter 6 (pp.90–100) of *How to Pass National 5 English* by David Swinney (ISBN 9781444182095).

Text 4 – Prose – *In Church* by Iain Crichton Smith

Question	Expected response	Max. mark	Additional guidance
29	Candidates should explain how the language used makes clear how much the speaker dislikes army life. Reference (1) Comment/explanation (1) × 2	4	Possible answers include: ■ 'forced' (1) suggests he was under compulsion, it was against his will (1) ■ 'what they call' (1) implies he doesn't agree (1) ■ his outlook ('gaze') (1) was different from the army's (1) ■ 'despised' (1) suggests he looked down on them with contempt (1) ■ 'feared' (1) suggests it caused him alarm (1) ■ list of the men's shortcomings (1) emphasises how many there were (1) ■ 'fornicated' (1) suggests immoral behaviour (1) ■ 'spat' (1) suggests disgusting, unhealthy behaviour (1) ■ 'filthily' (1) suggests lack of hygiene, lack of self-respect (1)
30	Candidates should explain two ways in which the writer uses contrast to emphasise the strangeness of the Christmas truce. Contrast (1 + 1) × 2 Award condensed answers.	4	Possible answers include: ■ contrasts the horrors of war (1) with a friendly/sociable game of football (1) ■ contrasts the horrors of war (1) with the sociable activity of sharing photographs (1) ■ contrasts civilised behaviour of German officer (1) with the bombardment to follow (1) ■ contrasts the banality of looking at watch (1) with horrors to come (1)
31	Candidates should explain in their own words as far as possible why the speaker is angry at God. Each point (1) × 4	4	Possible answers include: ■ used to think God was on the side of the innocent (1) ■ God is no longer on the side of the innocent (1) ■ believes God is 'absent' (1) ■ God has left him alone to suffer (1) ■ God has left the world to suffer (1) ■ God doesn't care (1) ■ God has allowed mankind to engage in the destruction of war (1)

Question	Expected response	Max. mark	Additional guidance
32	Candidates should show how Crichton Smith creates tension between characters. Reference could be made to the following: ■ **'In Church':** tension between Colin Macleod and the 'preacher' ■ **'The Telegram':** tension between the two women ■ **'Mother and Son':** tension between mother and son ■ **'The Painter':** tension between Red Roderick and his father-in-law; between the narrator and William; between William and the community ■ **'The Red Door':** tension between Murdo and the community; between Murdo and Mary ■ **'The Crater':** tension between Robert and Sgt Smith; between Robert and his men	8	Marks for this question should be allocated following the guidelines given at the start of these Marking Instructions.

Text 5 – Prose – *Zimmerobics* by Anne Donovan

Question	Expected response	Max. mark	Additional guidance
33	Candidates should show how the narrator's physical discomfort is conveyed. Reference (1) Comment/explanation (1) × 2	4	Possible answers include: ■ 'jaggy pains' (1) suggests she experiences sharp bursts of pain (1) ■ 'vertebrae grinding' (1) suggests her bones are crunching, grating against each other (1) ■ onomatopoeic 'clicking and crunking' (1) suggests rattling, noisy, malfunctioning (1) ■ simile 'like the central heating boiler starting up' (1) suggests (light-heartedly) she is a cumbersome machine (1)
34	Candidates should explain two impressions they are given of Catherine's personality. Aspect of personality (1) Reference/justification (1) × 2	4	Possible answers include: ■ not interested in aunt (1) minimal response of 'Uh-huh' (1) ■ obsessively tidy (1) 'busy rearranging ornaments on the mantelpiece' (1) ■ unsympathetic (1) 'gave me one of her looks' (1) ■ great believer in virtue of activity (1) 'I should take more interest' (1) ■ persistent (1) 'always trying to get me' (1) ■ brisk, bossy (1) has organised TV for aunt unasked (1) **or** her habit of speaking in short, curt sentences (1)

Question	Expected response	Max. mark	Additional guidance
35	Candidates should show how the writer conveys the contrast between the narrator and her niece. Aspect of contrast (1) Reference(s) (1)	4	Possible answers include: ■ aunt is content to do nothing, while niece has no time for inactivity (1) 'daydream'/'lost inside my own head' and/or 'not in her nature to daydream …' (1) ■ aunt has forgotten about film when Catherine next visits, while it's the first thing niece asks about (1) 'I was caught off my guard' and/or 'Did you enjoy the film?' (1) ■ aunt has no interest in being sociable, while niece thinks meeting people is important (1) 'I'd rather just sit here' and/or 'go and meet people' (1) ■ aunt is content 'inside my own head', while niece criticises her for having no interest in 'anything outside yourself' (2) ■ aunt is not bothered about order or routine, while niece is like a 'stapler', suggesting she is functional, mechanical, controlling (2)
36	Candidates should show how the theme of conflict between characters is explored. Reference could be made to the following: ■ **'Zimmerobics':** between Miss Knight and her niece ■ **'Away in a Manger':** between mother and daughter over homeless man ■ **'Dear Santa':** between narrator and sister; between narrator and mother ■ **'All That Glisters':** between narrator and Aunt Pauline ■ **'A Chitterin Bite':** between child narrator and friend; between adult narrator and lover ■ **'Virtual Pals':** between the two correspondents over such matters as relationships, language, feminism	8	Marks for this question should be allocated following the guidelines given at the start of these Marking Instructions.

C

Text 1 – Poetry – *Mrs Midas* by Carol Ann Duffy

Question	Expected response	Max. mark	Additional guidance
37	Candidates should explain how the poet creates a light-hearted, humorous tone. Reference/selection of example (1) Comment/explanation (1) × 2	4	Possible answers include: ■ 'keep his hands to himself' (1) normally a criticism of someone making unwanted advances, but here emphasising the need for him not to touch anything (lest it turn to gold) (1) ■ 'The toilet I didn't mind' (1) having taken precautions with the cat and the phone, she appears not to mind the prospect of sitting on a gold toilet (1) ■ '... we all have wishes; granted./But who has wishes granted?' (1) wordplay involving two takes on 'wishes granted' (1. = I accept that everyone makes wishes; 2. = nobody actually has them come true) (1) ■ 'you'll be able to give up smoking for good' (1) the fact that he is unable to light a cigarette (because it turns to gold) leads her to joke that now he'll (finally) be able to stop smoking (1)
38	Candidates should show how the poet's use of language conveys the way the relationship between the speaker and her husband has changed. Reference (1) Comment/explanation (1) × 2 (i.e. 1 from 'before'; 1 from 'now')	4	Possible answers include: Now: ■ 'Separate beds' (1) minor sentence to suggest the simplicity (inevitability) of the change to less intimacy (1) ■ 'put a chair against my door' (1) suggests fear, need for protection (1) ■ 'near petrified' (1) suggests state of heightened fear (1) ■ 'turning the spare room/into the tomb of Tutankhamun' (1) slightly jokey reference suggests an element of contempt (1) ■ 'feared his honeyed embrace' (1) suggests she is frightened of him, of the possible effect on her (1) ■ 'turn my lips to a work of art' (1) suggests that something alive, capable of showing love, will become something inanimate (1) Before: ■ 'passionate' (1) suggests loving, fervent relationship (1) ■ 'halcyon days' (1) suggests a glorious, heavenly, untroubled time (1) ■ 'unwrapping each other' (1) suggests sensual, loving, intimate process (1) ■ 'rapidly' (1) suggests uncontrolled desire (1) ■ 'like presents' (1) suggests generosity, reciprocal love, warmth, happiness (1) ■ 'fast food' (1) suggests simple, guilty pleasure (1)

Question	Expected response	Max. mark	Additional guidance
39	Candidates should explain how the speaker's fears are conveyed. Reference (1) Comment/explanation (1) × 2	4	Possible answers include: ■ 'its perfect ore limbs' (1) suggests the baby's arms/legs are inanimate, lifeless (1) ■ 'tongue/like a precious latch' (1) suggests tongue (connotations of speech/kissing) is inanimate, concerned with fastening, obstructing entry (1) ■ 'amber eyes/holding their pupils like flies' (1) suggests lifelessness, distortion of the human, restriction of key sense of sight (1) ■ 'dream-milk/burned in my breasts' (1) suggests pain, thwarting of maternal of love (1)
40	Candidates should show how Duffy explores tension within a relationship or within an individual. Reference could be made to the following: ■ **'Mrs Midas':** tension within relationship with husband; tension in her own mind at the end: she misses him physically ■ **'Originally':** tension within the family (brothers' complaints and parents' anxiety); tension within herself over 'where she comes from' ■ **'War Photographer':** tension between photographer and the newspaper readers; tension in his own mind about the nature of the images he captures ■ **'Havisham':** tension in attitude to 'Beloved sweetheart bastard'; tension in own mind as she plots revenge ■ **'Anne Hathaway':** some sense that the intensity of the relationship creates a kind of positive, rewarding tension; tension between lovers' exhilaration and the guests' dullness ■ **'Valentine':** relationships seen as poisonous/dangerous, doomed to fail; tension between the conventional and the unconventional	8	Marks for this question should be allocated following the guidelines given at the start of these Marking Instructions.

Text 2 – Poetry – *Trio* by Edwin Morgan

Question	Expected response	Max. mark	Additional guidance
41	Candidates should explain how the poet establishes a happy mood at the start of the poem. Reference (1) Comment (1) × 2	4	Possible answers include: ■ 'Christmas lights' (1) bright and cheerful, association with festivity, celebration (1) ■ 'the three of them are laughing' (1) everyone is in a good mood (1) ■ 'a cloud of happiness' (1) even their breath is associated with joy (1) ■ 'Wait till he sees this but!' (1) suggests a sense of anticipation, pleasure in giving (1)
42	Candidates should explain how the poet's use of language creates an effective description of any two from the chihuahua, the baby, and the guitar. Reference (1) Comment (1) × 2	4	Possible answers include: the chihuahua: ■ 'tiny' (1) suggests cute, appealing, vulnerable (1) ■ 'Royal Stewart tartan' (1) suggests colourful, perhaps a little dignified (1) ■ 'coat like a teapot-holder' (1) suggests something a little ridiculous, incongruous (1) the baby: ■ 'white shawl' (1) suggests clean, pure (1) ■ 'all bright eyes' (1) suggests radiant, alert (1) ■ 'mouth like favours' (1) like a good luck charm (1) ■ 'in a fresh sweet cake' (1) suggests sweet, appealing, nourishing (1) the guitar: ■ 'swells out' (1) suggests it is like something alive, organic (1) ■ 'silver tinsel tape' (1) suggests bright, associated with decoration and with giving (1) ■ 'brisk sprig of mistletoe' (1) associated with celebration, mystical powers (1)
43	Candidates should explain in their own words the poet's feelings about what he has just seen. Each point (1) × 4 Reference/quotation is not necessary.	4	Possible answers include: ■ they are objects of wonder/admiration (1) ■ they are a celebration of life (1) ■ they render Christ's birth in a sense irrelevant (1) ■ they have the power to defy death (1) ■ they are united like a conquering army (1) ■ they can overcome any threat (1) ■ they create positive feelings (1) ■ they uplift/inspire him (1) ■ they create feelings of confidence, safety (1) ■ they cause him to feel saddened, depressed (1)

Question	Expected response	Max. mark	Additional guidance
44	Candidates should show how Morgan transforms a simple event or situation into something special and thought-provoking. Reference could be made to the following: ■ **'Trio'**: sight of three people with Christmas gifts prompts reflection on meaning of Christmas, the nature of giving ■ **'Good Friday'**: encounter on a bus leads to reflection on education, religion ■ **'In the Snack-bar'**: encounter in the snack-bar leads to reflection on the life of the blind man ■ **'Slate'**: description of a geological feature leads to reflection on aspects of nationality ■ **'Hyena'**: focus on one animal leads to reflection on relationship between man and nature ■ **'Winter'**: the sight of a frozen pond leads to reflections on death, decay in nature	8	Marks for this question should be allocated following the guidelines given at the start of these Marking Instructions.

Text 3 – Poetry – *Visiting Hour* by Norman MacCaig

Question	Expected response	Max. mark	Additional guidance
45	Candidates should explain how the speaker's discomfort is made clear. Reference (1) Comment (1) × 2	4	Possible answers include: ■ 'combs my nostrils' (1) sense of irritation, intrusion (1) ■ 'bobbing along' (1) suggests uneven movement (1) ■ 'green and yellow corridors' (1) association with sickness, nausea (1) ■ 'seems a corpse' (1) suggests he is uncertain, disorientated (1) ■ 'vanishes' (1) creates a sense of mystery, dislocation (1) ■ 'I will not feel, I will not/feel, until/I have to' (1) jerky rhythm conveys tension, disorientation (1)

Question	Expected response	Max. mark	Additional guidance
46	Candidates should show how the speaker's admiration for the nurses is conveyed. Technique/reference (1) Comment (1) × 2	4	Possible answers include: ■ repetition of adverbs: 'walk lightly, swiftly' (1) admires their ability to deal with stresses of nursing (1) ■ unusual word order: 'here and up and down and there' (1) suggests their ability to be in many places, perform a range of tasks (1) ■ word choice/metaphor: 'slender waists miraculously carrying their burden' (1) suggests he admires their ability to deal with stresses/burdens despite being small/light (1) ■ word choice: 'miraculously' (1) suggests they have angelic, magical powers (1) ■ repetition: 'so much pain, so/many deaths …/ so many farewells' (1) suggests they have to deal with pain and death frequently (1)
47	Candidates should explain how an image adds to their understanding of the poem. Reference (1) Comment (1)	2	Possible answers include: ■ 'white cave of forgetfulness' (1) comparison of room to a 'cave' conveys idea of seclusion, isolation from rest of world (1) ■ 'trembles on its stalk' (1) comparison of arm to 'stalk' conveys its thinness, fragility (1) ■ 'a glass fang is fixed,/not guzzling but giving' (1) comparison of drip to a 'fang' creates ghoulish/slightly amusing idea of vampire in reverse (1) ■ 'the distance of pain' (1) suggests that pain can in some way be measured and that he is aware of how much she is suffering (1)
48	Candidates should comment on the effectiveness of the last three lines as a conclusion to the poem. Comment (1) Reference (1)	2	Possible answers include: ■ sense of sadness, futility (1) summed up in oxymoron of 'fruitless fruits' (1) ■ imminence of patient's death (1) seen in 'books that will not be read' (1) ■ sense of helplessness (1) emphasised in use of 'only' (1)

Question	Expected response	Max. mark	Additional guidance
49	Candidates should show how MacCaig conveys deep personal feelings. Reference could be made to the following: ■ **'Visiting Hour':** sense of loss, deep affection, of his own helplessness ■ **'Memorial':** sense of grief, loss, love ■ **'Sounds of the Day':** sense of loss, shock, numbness ■ **'Aunt Julia':** sense of love, admiration, loss ■ **'Assisi':** sense of sympathy (beggar); contempt (tourists/ priest), anger (Church) ■ **'Basking Shark':** sense of wonder, questioning of own place in the scheme of things	8	Marks for this question should be allocated following the guidelines given at the start of these Marking Instructions.

There is further practical guidance on the poetry of Norman MacCaig in chapter 6 (pp.72–89) of *How to Pass National 5 English* by David Swinney (ISBN 9781444182095).

Text 4 – Poetry – *My Grandmother's Houses* by Jackie Kay

Question	Expected response	Max. mark	Additional guidance
50	Candidates should identify four aspects of the grandmother's personality. Each point (1) × 4 Textual reference not required.	4	Possible answers include: ■ she is a hard/conscientious worker (1) ■ she dominates her granddaughter/is frequently giving orders (1) ■ she is subservient to/in awe of/afraid of her 'betters' (1) ■ she is not well educated/lacks sophistication (1) ■ she wants her granddaughter to be seen in a good light (1) ■ she is a strict/violent disciplinarian (1)
51	Candidates should choose one example of imagery from lines 4–7 and explain what it suggests about what is being described. Reference (1) Comment (1)	2	Possible answers include: ■ 'like an octopus's arms' (to describe the way the rooms lead off the hall) (1) suggests a large number/going in all directions/a bit scary (1) ■ 'a one-winged creature' (to describe the grand piano) (1) makes the piano seem alive, a little mysterious (1)

Question	Expected response	Max. mark	Additional guidance
52	Candidates should explain how the poet conveys the personality of 'the woman'. Reference (1) Comment (1) × 3	6	Possible answers include: ■ 'posh' (1) suggests she is/thinks she is superior/of a higher class (1) ■ 'all smiles' (1) suggests she is insincere/putting on a show (1) ■ 'Would you like ...' (1) suggests she is (superficially at least) kindly (1) ■ 'Lovely'/'beautiful' (1) suggests she is (superficially at least) encouraging/friendly (1) ■ 'Lovely'/'beautiful' (1) suggests she is patronising (1) ■ 'skin the colour of café au lait' (1) suggests she is insensitive, verging on racist (1) ■ 'skin the colour of café au lait' (1) suggests she is not very PC (politically correct) (1) ■ 'You just get back to your work' (1) suggests she is high-handed, officious, haughty (1)
53	Candidates should show how Jackie Kay creates vivid impressions of people. Reference could be made to the following: ■ **'My Grandmother's Houses':** the speaker, the grandmother, the woman ■ **'Bed':** the speaker ■ **'Lucozade':** the speaker and the mother ■ **'Gap Year':** the speaker, her father ■ **'Divorce':** the speaker, her parents (as seen through her eyes) ■ **'Keeping Orchids':** the speaker, the birth mother (as seen through her eyes)	8	Marks for this question should be allocated following the guidelines given at the start of these Marking Instructions.

Section 2 – Critical Essay

If minimum standards have been achieved, then the supplementary marking grid will allow you to place the work on a scale of marks out of 20.

Once an essay has been judged to have met minimum standards, it does not have to meet all the suggestions for it to fall into a band of marks. More typically, there will be a spectrum of strengths and weaknesses which span bands.

Marking Principles for the Critical Essay are as follows:

- The essay should first be read to establish whether it achieves relevance and the standards for technical accuracy outlined in the supplementary marking grid.
- If minimum standards are not achieved, the maximum mark which can be awarded is 9.
- If minimum standards have been achieved, then the supplementary marking grid will allow you to place the work on a scale of marks out of 20.

NB Using the supplementary marking grid:

Bands are not grades. The five bands are designed primarily to assist with placing each candidate response at an appropriate point on a continuum of achievement. Assumptions about final grades or association of final grades with particular bands should not be allowed to influence objective assessment.

Supplementary marking grid

	20–18	17–14	13–10	9–5	4–0
The candidate demonstrates	• a **high degree of familiarity** with the text as a whole • **very good understanding** of the central concerns of the text • a line of thought that is **consistently relevant** to the task	• **familiarity** with the text as a whole • **good understanding** of the central concerns of the text • a line of thought that is **relevant** to the task	• **some familiarity** with the text as a whole • **some understanding** of the central concerns of the text • a line of thought that is **mostly relevant** to the task	• **familiarity with some aspects** of the text • **attempts** a line of thought **but this may lack relevance to the task**	Although such essays should be rare, in this category, the candidate's essay will demonstrate one or more of the following • it contains numerous errors in spelling/grammar/punctuation/sentence construction/paragraphing • knowledge and understanding of the text(s) are not used to answer the question • any analysis and evaluation attempted are unconvincing • the answer is simply too thin
Analysis of the text demonstrates	• **thorough awareness** of the writer's techniques, through analysis, making **confident** use of critical terminology • **very detailed/thoughtful** explanation of stylistic devices supported by a **range of well-chosen** references and/or quotations	• **sound awareness** of the writer's techniques through analysis, making **good** use of critical terminology • **detailed explanation** of stylistic devices supported by **appropriate** references and/or quotations	• **an awareness** of the writer's techniques through analysis, making **some** use of critical terminology • explanation of stylistic devices supported by **some appropriate** references and/or quotations	• **some awareness of the more obvious** techniques used by the writer • **description of some** stylistic devices followed by some reference and/or quotation	
Evaluation of the text is shown through	• a **well-developed** commentary of what has been enjoyed/gained from the text(s), supported by a **range** of well-chosen references to its **relevant** features	• a **reasonably developed** commentary of what has been enjoyed/gained from the text(s), supported by **appropriate** references to its **relevant** features	• **some** commentary of what has been enjoyed/gained from the text(s), supported by **some appropriate** references to its **relevant** features	• **brief** commentary of what has been enjoyed/gained from the text(s), followed by **brief** reference to its features	
The candidate	• uses language to communicate a line of thought **very clearly** • uses spelling, grammar, sentence construction and punctuation which are **consistently** accurate • structures the essay **effectively to enhance** meaning/purpose • uses paragraphing which is **accurate and effective**	• uses language to communicate a line of thought **clearly** • uses spelling, grammar, sentence construction and punctuation which are **mainly** accurate • structures the essay **very well** • uses paragraphing which is **accurate**	• uses language to communicate a line of thought **at first reading** • uses spelling, grammar, sentence construction and punctuation which are **sufficiently** accurate • attempts to structure the essay **in an appropriate way** • uses paragraphing which is **sufficiently accurate**	• uses language to communicate a line of thought which may be disorganised and/or difficult to follow • makes some errors in spelling/grammar/sentence construction/punctuation • has not structured the essay well • has made some errors in paragraphing	
In summary, the candidate's essay is	Thorough and precise	Very detailed and shows some insight	Fairly detailed and accurate	Lacks detail and relevance	Superficial and/or technically weak

Acknowledgements

The Publishers would like to thank the following for permission to reproduce copyright material:

Pages **3–4**, the article 'Sport will continue to transcend the ages' by Matthew Syed, taken from *TheTimes* August 12, 2015. Used with permission from The Times UK.

pages **7–8**, **33–34** and **59–60**, extracts from 'Bold Girls' by Rona Munro, used with permission from Nick Hern Books Ltd.

pages **8–10**, **34–35** and **60–61**, extracts from 'Sailmaker' by Alan Spence, reproduced by permission of Hodder Education.

pages **10–11**, **36–37** and **62–63**, extracts from 'Tally's Blood' by Ann Marie Di Mambro reproduced by permission of Ann Marie Di Mambro/Hodder Education (first published by Learning and Teaching Scotland, 2002, then by Education Scotland).

pages **12–13**, **38–39** and **65–66**, extracts from 'The Cone-Gatherers' by Robin Jenkins, used by permission of Canongate Books Ltd.

pages **13–14**, **39–40** and **66–67**, extracts from 'The Testament of Gideon Mack' © James Robertson, reproduced by permission of United Agents LLP on behalf of the author and by permission of Penguin Books Ltd.

pages **14–15**, **41–42** and **68–69**, extract from 'Kidnapped' by Robert Louis Stevenson, published by Cassell and Company Ltd 1886 – public domain.

page **16**, extract from 'The Telegram'; pages **42–43** extract from 'Mother and Son'; pages **69–70** extract from 'In Church' by Ian Crichton Smith, taken from 'The Red Door: The Complete English Stories 1949–76'. Reproduced by permission of Birlinn Ltd.

Pages **17–18**, extract from 'Virtual Pals'; pages **44–45** extract from 'Away in a Manger'; pages **70–71** extract from 'Zimmerobics' by Anne Donovan, taken from 'Hieroglyphics: and Other Stories', 2001. Used by permission of Canongate Books Ltd.

Page **19**, 'Originally' taken from 'The Other Country' (Anvil Press Poetry, 1990); page **46** 'Anne Hathaway', originally published in 'The World's Wife' (Macmillan 1999); page **72**, extract from 'Mrs Midas' originally published in 'The World's Wife' (Macmillan, 1999) © Carol Ann Duffy. Reproduced by permission of the author c/o Rogers, Coleridge & White Ltd, 20 Powis Mews, London, W11 1JN.

Pages **20–21**, 'In the Snack-bar'; page **47**, 'Hyena'; pages **73–74** 'Trio' by Edwin Morgan, extracts taken from 'Collected Poems', reproduced by permission Carcanet Press Limited.

Pages **21–22**, 'Assisi'; page **48** 'Basking Shark'; pages **74–75** 'Visiting Hour' by Norman MacCaig, poems taken from 'The Poems of Norman MacCaig', 2011. Reproduced by permission of Birlinn Ltd.

Page **23**, 'Keeping Orchids'; pages **49–50** 'Lucozade'; pages **76–77** 'My Grandmother's Houses' by Jackie Kay, taken from 'Darling: New & Selected Poems' (Bloodaxe Books, 2007) reprinted by permission of Bloodaxe Books on behalf of the author.

Pages **29–30**, extract adapted from the article 'The Real Price of Gold' by Brook Larmer in *National Geographic Magazine* (2009), Volume 215, Issue 1. Used by permission of the National Geographic Society.

Pages **55–56**, the article 'Why Didn't People Smile in Old Photographs? You Asked Google – and Here's the Answer', by Jonathan Jones in the *Guardian*, August 12 2015, Copyright © Guardian News & Media Ltd 2016.